Rock Queen

Rock Queen

Major ascents from the world
famous French climber

Catherine Destivelle

Translated from French by
Marguerite Wright

HAYLOFT PUBLISHING LTD

Published by Hayloft Publishing Ltd., 2015
First published as *Ascensions*, © Flammarion, Paris, 2012

Hayloft Publishing Ltd, South Stainmore,
Kirkby Stephen, Westmorland, CA17 4DJ

tel: 07971 352473
email: books@hayloft.eu
web: www.hayloft.eu

ISBN 978 1 910237 07 6

A CIP record for this book is available from The British Library

Papers used by Hayloft are natural, recyclable products made from wood
grown in sustainable forests. The manufacturing processes conform to the
environmental regulations of the country of origin.

Designed, printed and bound in the EU

CONTENTS

Foreword by Doug Scott   vii
Introduction by Jim Curran   ix
Notes on Translation   xii
Preface   1
A passion is born   14
Climbing becomes a profession   48
Return to the mountains: The Trango Towers
                       and the Bonatti Pillar   87
The Dru: a first   105
Colour plates   113
Solo up the Eiger in winter   157
Les Grandes Jorasses and the Matterhorn   185
Conclusion   208

ROCK QUEEN

FOREWORD

THE most important thing to say is that in the last 20 years Catherine Destivelle has become one of the most famous women climbers in the world.

It's not just that she is a female climber; she has done things that no-one has done before and, in her own right she is a brilliant climber. Catherine has been recognised as world champion of free climbing many times.

Certainly for Catherine I'll remember 1992 and the solo of the Eiger's north face in seventeen hours – it was just amazing – and then to put a new route solo on the south west pillar of the Dru (the Bonatti Pillar). She has an insatiable appetite for adventure, which almost cost her her life when she fell into a glacier while climbing in Antarctica.

She has also taken part in the big debates about protecting the environment of the mountains and she's very hot on over-bolting and tooling rocks, wanting to keep climbing pure and the challenges as they've always been for future generations. Catherine's played a part in that environmental debate and is now putting something back into mountaineering as she recently became a publisher with Bruno Dupety at Les Editions du Mont Blanc, specialising in books about climbing and climbers.

When you see her in Chamonix, in a crowded room, you can see how modest she is – she's quiet and unassuming, rather different from some of her male colleagues!

She has earned huge respect amongst all the British climbing fraternity and was recently guest of honour at the Alpine Club. Climbers hold her in the highest esteem and whenever she comes over here to give a lecture the venues are always full. She's a climber's climber.

This book is a first translation into English and tells Catherine's story from her rebellious youth – finding an outlet in climbing – this is something she has in common with many climbers who were difficult young people until they found climbing to channel their energies.

It is a frank story, not shying away from difficulties whether personal or on a rock face. Catherine tackles problems face to rock face, studies them and climbs over them or around them. Above all this book is about Catherine's enduring love of mountains and wild places.

Doug Scott, CBE
written on the banks of the River Spey, Scotland
September 2015

INTRODUCTION

WHEN I first visited the French Alps in 1964, the prevailing ethos probably owed more to the 1930s than the 1960s. True, many shops in Chamonix displayed the stunning mountain photos of Pierre Tiarraz and everywhere, it seemed, were glossy photographs of French pin-up boy Gaston Rebuffat posing self-consciously in his trademark red guides' jersey, big boots and white socks, poised over impressive voids with Mont Blanc in the background.

However, the average impoverished British climber viewed the French with deep suspicion and occasionally outright hostility. This was reciprocated (most of all by the shopkeepers of Chamonix) and, with a few famous exceptions, there was not much love lost between the two communities, and is best summed up by Ian McNaught-Davis in his famous article 'Deux Grandes Bieres', a masterpiece of British climbing humour.

In the mountains we thought the French were far too cavalier in their use of direct aid on routes that could obviously be climbed free, and they in turn found the Brits climbed so slowly they often had to bivouac on quite minor climbs. Both sides had a point and mutual suspicion and jealousy continued into the 1980s when there was a real meeting of minds.

This was due in part to an explosion of spectacular high quality French films, often set in the Verdon Gorge in Provence and featuring the stunning solo climbs of Patrick Edlinger. The films came as a shock to the complacent Brits who belatedly realised that free climbing standards in France were as high as or higher than our own; though there was some residual aggro for the French over use of expansion bolts, still outlawed on the sacred British rock.

But then, in 1984, a young French woman had the audacity to climb Right Wall on Dinas Cromlech, one of the hardest climbs in Britain at the time. The perpetrator was, of course, Catherine Destivelle. Since then Catherine has gone from strength to strength, at times achieving almost superstar status. Her most popular film *Seo* set in Mali, West Africa, was screened on British TV, and even today, I am occasionally asked if I knew 'that beautiful French girl who climbs without ropes?'

I had known Catherine vaguely through film festivals and conferences but it was not until a film festival in Dundee in 1996 that we got talking, and I first mooted the idea of making a film with her. Ever charming and (I thought) not wanting to reject the idea out of hand, she giggled 'Why not – we'll see!'

And so it came to pass that in the summer of 1997 we, together with a small film crew and her then husband, Erik Decamp, spent a memorable week filming on the Old Man of Hoy, an adventure made all the more special because Catherine was three months pregnant. We called the film *Rock Queen* and it is also the name of this autobiography.

I have been asked countless times, 'what's she really like?' Though I have come to know her fairly well and am proud to call her a friend, it is a question I find hard to answer. She is (obviously) extrovert, friendly and extremely attractive. She has a reserve that is hard to penetrate and though her English is excellent, it is still, to her, a foreign language. Although we meet infrequently, as climbers often do, it is a friendship that has lasted over twenty years.

Despite making her name as a solo climber, she is a highly competent and experienced mountaineer (you don't solo the North Face of the Eiger in winter in a day without a huge background of mountaineering experience). When we were together on the Old Man of Hoy I was constantly impressed by her emphasis on safety; as she told the camera 'I do not want to die.' On the subject of soloing she worried that nobody should do it too much – it can give you a false sense of security (not for me, I hasten to add).

In the book Catherine tells a selective story of her adventures in such a matter of fact way that the reader shouldn't under-estimate her achievements. The description of her accident in Antarctica when she broke her leg on the summit of an unclimbed peak is told so simply that the reader might be left unaware that it was an epic that rivals much better known and high profile stories.

Throughout the book she tells her stories with becoming modesty. It is tempting for me to give a blow-by-blow critique of the contents, but that would rather miss the point, which is to encourage you to read the whole book.

Catherine Destivelle 'La Belle Catherine', has deservedly become one of the world's most famous climbers. The following pages tell you why.

Jim Curran, Sheffield, 2015.

NOTES ON TRANSLATION

IN the original French, Catherine Destivelle lets the reader get to know her with a narrative which combines colloquial expressions and a smattering of slang with a much more formal, correct, literary style using a very wide vocabulary. The voice and sense of humour of this well educated woman shine through her words. To some extent, her way of expressing herself is closer to the directness of the Anglo-Saxon mind than a more formal French literary style.

In translation, I have tried to maintain the voice, humour and informality of the author. I have stopped short of using abbreviations, except in direct speech. Catherine herself does not cross the line from 'correct' literary French; despite the colloquialisms, she uses the literary tenses which would not be employed in speech.

Although received wisdom is that the English language has more words than the French, that does not take into account the wealth of slang which a French native speaker has at their disposal. It is a whole parallel language and could be likened to London Cockney rhyming slang which seems to have an alternative to any verb or noun. Yet an English writer would hardly pepper their narrative with rhyming slang. With a few exceptions, where emotions were running high, Catherine has used no swear words. In English, I have frequently resorted to other ways of expressing the informal colloquial style.

It was sometimes challenging to describe Catherine's emotions. One of the things which makes this book so enjoyable is how frankly this astonishingly self-disciplined woman shares her feelings and admits to tears. The famous 'stiff upper lip' prevents the English speaker from talking about emotion in general terms without explanation. On occasion, I took the liberty of being a little more precise than Catherine about whether her emotion was terror, apprehension, shock, exhaustion... I hope she will forgive me.

If the French talk about their states of mind in general terms, where anything medical or technical is concerned, more detail is shared than in English. Climbers speaking English are normally more economical with their vocabulary. 'Protection' or 'pro' covers a multitude of possibilities for example, as does 'belay'. Catherine tends to give more detail about the equipment she was using on her ascents. I hope English readers will find it informative.

There were a few instances where cultural references could not be translated but readers might like an explanation. When young, foolish and paralysed with fear on a shifting scree slope from which she had picked plants to make *Genepi,* a type of vermouth aperitif drink, which tastes sharply herby, Catherine describes herself as acting out an episode of Bécassine: *Bécassine goes to the mountains.* This was one of the first ever serialised cartoon characters in France at the beginning of the last century. The eponymous heroine is shown as a girl in peasant clothes. She is a sort of Laurel and Hardyesque character for whom nothing ever goes right.

When Catherine was in her tent trying without success to concentrate on her reading, the novel in question was *La Fée Carabine* which translates as 'The Fairy Gunmother.' This is the second of a bizarre and hilarious sequence of novels by best-selling French author Daniel Pennac. It recounts the exploits and extraordinary family life of one Benjamin Malaussène who lives in the Belleville district of Paris. The books are written with a jaw-droppingly wide and rich use of Parisian slang.

French readers will be aware that the young men Catherine climbed with in the early days seem to have studied at the most prestigious institutions for the sciences. Their degrees would have opened doors into the higher echelons of French society if they were not already from that 'milieu'.

I have mostly left the way Catherine expresses herself un-changed, so that her own voice can be heard. If at times the language seems less concise than one would expect from a na-tive English speaker, I would ask the gentle reader to imagine a slight French accent...

ABOUT THE TRANSLATOR

Marguerite Wright was born in London. When her parents, of German Jewish origin, chose her French name, it was merely because they liked it but she has spent most of her life creating real French links for herself. A school exchange with an artistic Parisian family, who welcomed her as one of their own, let her taste freedom never allowed by her own over-protective par-ents; she acquired a lifelong love for all things French and friendships which endure to this day. When her French 'family' moved to the High Alps, she frequently visited them there and may well have taken one of the same overnight trains from Paris to Gap as young Catherine Destivelle.

While Catherine escaped from the Paris suburbs to her beloved mountains at every opportunity, feeling that she did not fit in with her classmates, schoolgirl Marguerite left sub-urban London to be with her Parisian friends. Educated at North London Collegiate School, Marguerite supplemented 'A' level classroom French during term-time with an impres-sive acquisition of slang from the London Soho French club where she spent her weekends dancing 'le rock' and helping backstage with drama. By the time she went on to trendy Sus-sex University for a degree in French Studies, she was fluent enough to wangle her way into the bi-lingual section.

She spent a year as assistant in Lyon; handy for skiing in the Alps. After her studies, she lived in Pau, where she fell in love with the Pyrenees; much gentler mountains. Although she expected to stay in France, jobs took her and her boyfriend to live in Italy, Greece, Norway and Egypt in each of which country Marguerite gained a working knowledge of the lan-guage and cuisine. They eventually returned to England, where their two daughters grew up.

In addition to translating, Marguerite has worked in publishing, public relations, education and tourism. She currently works as a multi-lingual tourist guide at The Royal Pavilion and the Château de Selles-sur-Cher. Passionate about horticulture and heritage, she maintains her own large garden and volunteers in historic ones in two countries. For the last twelve years she, her husband, and their huge, hairy French dog have divided their lives between homes in Brighton and the Loire Valley in France.

ROCK QUEEN

PREFACE

For if they fall, the one will lift up his fellow:
but woe to him that is alone when he falleth;
for he hath not another to help him up.

Ecclesiastes, IV, 10

THE mountain had no name; only its altitude had been mapped – 4,160 metres – and we were the first ever to set foot upon its summit. This was Antarctica; that vast, frozen continent devoid of all human life.

We had just climbed up here and were celebrating with a photograph to add to our collection. It needed to be a really good one; to give to the media, who would no doubt be talking about our tour of the Ellsworth mountain range and our new first. An image that could have been taken anywhere would be a shame. I struck a suitable pose but unfortunately it hid the mountains in the distance behind me and to get the perfect angle I needed to be slightly further away.

I took one step backwards without looking, sure that the ice on the slope was even but when I shifted my weight, my foot did not meet the solid surface expected. For a moment, trying to regain my balance, I windmilled my arms frantically; but in vain. Inexorably my body started to tip. Even before my back hit the ice I was screaming to my partner, Erik Decamp, 'The rope! Get the rope! Stop the rope!'

With his eye to the viewfinder had he seen what was happening? He was my only hope; I was moving too fast to do anything to stop myself from plummeting. That was when I remembered both that the rope was only attached to my ice

1

axes planted in the hard snow without much care and that to take the photograph, Erik had moved about three metres away from the precarious anchor. Would he be able to stop the rope without pulling everything out?

Now I really fell fast, twisting in a great somersault, and then landed hard on the slope. 'The rope.' I shouted again. My right leg felt strangely floppy; I hoped it was not what I suspected. Then once more I was violently thrown into the air.

As I hit for the third time a few metres further down, I got a brief glimpse of the dark, icy abyss. I thought, 'If he can't stop me now, this time it's all over.' My stupidity would have cost me my life; and even worse; I was going to pull Erik down this death slide with me.

Just as my tumbling seemed ever dizzier and more violent, the rope stopped my fall with a brutal jerk. I landed chin first. I was a bit dazed; it took me a few seconds to work out which way up I was; but relieved and happy that the nightmare was over at last. Realising I was hanging upside-down, I got my arms and legs the right way up hoping that nothing was broken but bright spots of blood on the ice made me suspicious. Where was it coming from? I hurt all over but nowhere in particular.

With shaking hands, I pulled up the hem of my right trouser leg and saw to my horror that I had a compound fracture; I could barely take it in. Practical as usual and in an attempt to make things seem less awful, I tried to assess the situation positively: the bone wasn't sticking out; the weight of my boot, in addition to the weight of the crampons, had pushed the leg back in line and the wound was not bleeding a great deal; in other words, the artery was untouched. That was lucky.

Just then Erik asked, 'Are you OK?'

'Open fracture,' I shouted back.

The mountains echoed to 'Oh shit!' and then there was a long silence. Under the circumstances, that was basically all that could be said.

I couldn't believe that I had a broken leg. I mustn't have, it just wasn't possible, not here in Antarctica, so far from any help. However was I going to get back down the mountain? I had an idea, a last hope born of desperation; if the fracture was horizontal, maybe I could actually put weight on it? Testing out my idea, I put my foot down, in its cramponed boot on the slope. Gritting my teeth, I tried once, twice. No, impossible, the pain was intolerable. There could be no doubt as to the severity of the breakage.

If the situation had not been so serious, I would have cried with rage; how could I have been so stupid? I only had a moment for self-pity, as a question from Erik brought me to my senses, 'Is it bleeding a lot?'

'No'

'Can you get back up?'

He was right; I had to move. In the time it took to get used to the idea, I replied that I could. After all, I didn't really have a choice. I couldn't stay where I was.

'Can you get back to the ridge where we left the route?'

That sounded as if it would be tricky. We had climbed up the mountain on the other side and the place he was talking about was about 30 metres to his left. That meant I would need to go left for 25 metres diagonally back up the icy face without any help. A moment's reflection helped me visualise how to tackle it.

By crawling up the slope, left hand armed with an ice axe Erik had sent down the rope to me and right hand clutching an ascender, I heaved myself up with difficulty. At the first heave, I found that my right shoulder hurt and I found a lump on it; not soft like a bruise but hard; there was a bone sticking out. Although relieved to find I could still use it – and under the present circumstances that was the main thing – I felt a stab of irritation, anticipating yet more surgery. However, the more I pulled myself up, the less my shoulder bothered me. I was absolutely focused on avoiding falling again; planting my axe and the tips of my left crampons firmly into the ice, I hauled furiously to avoid slipping at all costs. If that happened and the rope went sideways, I could expect a twenty metre pendulum, which in the state I was in would be no fun at all.

When at last I managed to reach the summit ridge, I heaved myself onto the crest and wedged myself astride it to wait for Erik who was still holding the rope 30 metres over to the left.

I now tried to take stock of the situation. Whichever way I looked at it, I just couldn't see how I was going to get out of this fix. If only this accident had happened in the Alps. I could have just sat back and calmly waited for the helicopter. Here, there was no way I could expect any rescue services. There were in fact some people on the continent of Antarctica; just not within 500 kilometres. Anyway we had not brought our radio which, weighing five kilos had been left behind at base camp, and even if we had been able to make contact, the rescue team did not have a helicopter, so in the time it took them to get up to me, I would have died of cold. There was an icy little wind; it was nine o'clock in the evening and, though the sun never actually sets in December at the South Pole, the temperature was falling.

If I waited, I risked dying. I thought how stupid it would be to die like this. I reminded myself of the famous English climber Doug Scott who had broken both ankles on The Ogre in the Himalaya. That hadn't killed him; he had managed to crawl back to base camp in agonising pain and, although his were not compound fractures, he had lost the use of both legs. At least I still had one which worked.

As soon as Erik reached me I asked, 'What are we going to do?'

'We'll go down.'

'Go down? But which way? How?' I asked somewhat anxiously. Despite having Doug as a role model, I couldn't bear the idea of moving a single muscle.

'By the route we came up. It's the only one we know.'

He was right and there was no point in hanging around here. No one would come to our aid. Erik's determination helped me get back some of my fighting spirit and I glanced at the mountain. We had climbed it in shadow so as not to get too hot and seeing it in sunlight now gave my spirits another boost. The ambiance would be less gloomy and the sun would warm me up.

The flicker of optimism was faint however, since the slightest movement caused me enormous pain and the bottom of my injured leg was just a dead weight, responsive only to the laws of gravity. Just to it get over the top of the ridge, I had to take my foot in both hands to move it in the right direction. Was I going to be able to survive that much pain, given that I had already been climbing for eleven hours? My greatest worry was that, if I lost consciousness, Erik would not be able to get me down.

'Do you think I'll manage it?' I asked mainly for reassurance.

'Of course you will.' He smiled back at me.

Poor man, he can't have felt much like smiling at a time like that. How furious I was with myself, to have landed him with such a herculean task. I was thoroughly spoiling our amazing trip to Antarctica.

First of all Erik took off my crampon, which risked catching on uneven surfaces. Then we cobbled together a makeshift splint – an ice axe on either side of the leg held together with straps. Next he gently paid out the rope to lower me down the face. The first jolt was hideously painful. A metre further down we removed the axes. What we had put together was far worse than nothing. The rounded handles and the straps wouldn't stay in place and were pressing on my injured leg in a way which was pure torture. Instead, we knotted a pullover around the wound and, to protect my hurt limb, I supported it from underneath with my good leg.

Then, facing the void with my back against the mountain, I guided Erik about the speed while he let me down further. The surface was extremely uneven and, even though my leg was no longer actually touching the face, the slightest bump was still terribly painful. Each time I thought I might black out. To keep going I made myself breathe deeply in and out, which helped me be less tense and to ride the pain. Twenty metres or so further and Erik suggested I find a place to stop. We only had one 50 metre rope, meaning we could only go 25 metres at a time, so he could abseil down to me.

By passing a sling around a rock and driving in a piton, I cobbled together a firm enough anchor and clipped on to it. That way Erik could use the rope without having to worry about my safety.

Condemned to dangling alone and wretched from this first belay, I wondered over and over again whether I was going to be able to keep going.

There would be much suffering ahead. There was a drop of 1,600 metres down the mountain, the first two thirds of which were steep and made up of rock and ice; they would be really hard to get down; particularly as, in order to avoid a big over-hang, we would be obliged to take a diagonal route. That meant preparing myself for hanging like a pendulum on the rope...

The rest involved a long ice couloir. But if I got as far as that I would nearly be saved...

I tried to clear my head of thoughts. To manage the pain and stop the waves of dizziness that were coming over me, I needed to stop thinking. I needed just to wait for Erik and concentrate on myself, my breathing and my body which I was trying to relax in order to conserve energy. It was hard to keep up this state of concentration and I was inwardly begging Erik to get there soon. I was afraid I would flunk it.

When he reached my level, Erik popped two sweets into my mouth as a pick-me-up, then he retrieved the rope and we did the same thing all over again.

The first three or four pitches were the worst. Subsequently the pain seemed more bearable. Perhaps I was getting used to it? In any case, I had no choice. Resigned to the pain, I started to notice other things; for example that I could hardly feel my extremities any more. Despite the sunshine, the air temperature was cold; it must have been between -20°C and -30°C. While I was concentrating on not passing out earlier, I had not been aware of it. On top of everything, it would be stupid to allow my hands and feet to freeze and so, although causing a lot of effort, I made myself keep moving my fingers and toes to warm them up at each belay point.

With each of us focused on what they had to do, our descent followed an even rhythm. We knew each other well enough to communicate without the need for much talking; just a look or a word would do. From time to time – approximately every two hours – when I felt about to lose consciousness, I would give a sign. Erik would immediately come and give me little slaps on the cheeks and fill my mouth with sweets; then each returned to their task. He was in charge of safety and the ropes; I concentrated on my pain and my physical state. That meant Erik had the lion's share: working the ropes was not easy and often, to save slings whenever a section was suitable, he climbed down.

After eight hours of descent, the sun disappeared and it became bitterly cold. The following eight hours seemed never-ending. The waits at the belays were hardest to bear. Staying still, my fatigue, the cold and the pain all came pressing in. Hanging from my makeshift anchors, I tried not to notice the time passing as I lay on the slope, on the snow and the ice, on the side of my good leg so that the straps of my harness didn't cut off my circulation… My only goal was to hang on until I got down. That demanded a constant and huge effort of willpower and I found that breathing exercises were the best way to keep alert.

During the last hours of the descent, I was mostly worried about my left foot; the one on which I was constantly putting my weight. Despite the toe wiggling, I couldn't feel them anymore. I reminded myself that although a broken leg could be mended, a frozen foot would be amputated…

No. I did not want that. From then on, I could think only of getting down as quickly as possible. For the last 600 metres of ice couloir and snow, I was beyond pain – I no longer told Erik to brake the rope and let him regulate the speed as he saw fit. When it got to the end, he gave a sign – thumbs down – and I drove my ice axe into the snow with both hands, lay on top of it and signed to him – thumbs up – and he came and joined me, drove in his axes, let me down and so on.

These moves continued one after the other in a perfect, rapid flow which was suddenly interrupted. In my haste to reach level ground and caught up in this routine, I had pulled my axe out of the snow, ready to let my body go down the slope, before Erik had time to create a good placement with his axes.

We got a real fright but it was not a disaster. Erik still had good reflexes even though he was so tired and he threw himself on his partly-stuck-in axe shouting, 'Wait. I'm not ready.' Having checked my fall, he turned to me smiling and said in a gentle tone 'Careful.' In the pathetic state I was in, he had not dared say any more but in any case he didn't need to. I felt guilty enough. Through my mistake, I had yet again nearly precipitated us off the mountain. I was well aware of all the work Erik was doing and I admired him for it… Despite the urgency, he had led this descent with care and efficiency, not once putting us in danger.

The incident intensified our caution as we continued on our long and painful journey. For all our efforts, as we descended, I could feel my strength progressively draining away. For the last belays, I was so weak that I could barely push the axe into the snow the ten centimetres needed to stop me sliding. My whole body, my mind and my eyes were riveted to the point of metal, in terror that this fragile anchor would give way. I barely dared to breathe whilst waiting for Erik to arrive and secure us firmly.

The final 100 metres were less steep and Erik could at last walk downhill forwards, letting me slide in front of him at the end of the rope. All I needed to do now was to guide my legs so that they didn't get stuck in the snow, but they inevitably hit all the bumps. Anyway, by this time I no longer cared about the pain; I was in such a hurry to get down.

The first thing I did when we reached the longed-for horizontal ice, was to pull off my left boot to rub my foot. It was a great relief to see the toes white at the tips and not, as I had feared, black. Even though the injured side didn't seem to be affected by the temperature, I asked Erik to take off the other boot. It is not a good idea to leave a wet foot inside a boot in extremely low temperatures. This turned out to be quite an operation, as the plastic had stiffened in the icy temperatures and was impossible to get open. In order to get my foot out gently, Erik had to cut open the boot. I realised that it broke my heart; they were such good boots. From my reaction, I felt that I must still have a bit of mental energy left, but didn't mention it to Erik, who would probably have found my attitude inappropriate. As far as I was concerned, I thought that still being able to care about my clothes augured well, though I was hardly out of the woods; the tent was a good hour's walk further

Watching Erik pull my boot to pieces, I imagined that he would then pull me over the ice to where we had camped and it came as a shock when he told me that he intended to go and fetch the sledge from the tent. Although I didn't let on, I was far from pleased; I would have to wait, alone, for him to get back. I was shivering. I was exhausted. I didn't know if I could hang on for two hours. What if I passed out? Would he get back before I fell asleep, never to wake up, overcome by the cold? Resolved to give survival my best shot, I watched him race off. The poor man was exhausted and I nearly shouted after him, 'No need to run, it'll be fine,' but I was really no longer strong enough to shout and, even if I had been, I don't know if I would have had the courage to do so. Deep down inside me I was pleading, 'Yes, run, run! Hurry back.'

Once he was out of earshot, sitting in that desert of ice, legs stretched in front of me, one foot pointing up to the sky and the other strangely tipped on its side, I felt like a child who had been abandoned in the middle of the road. Completely without inhibition, I let out a continuous noise whilst chattering my teeth, the way I used to when I was little and had swum in the North Sea. The sound reassured me; it proved I really was alive.

Goodness, how cold it was. I couldn't stop shivering. It was one o'clock in the afternoon and there was no hope of seeing the sun for another few hours. I thought back to what we had been doing the day before at the same time. We were climbing this nameless peak, happy to be out of the sun. It meant that we had set out 27 hours before, although it seemed an age ago. I had to hold on for another two, long hours. My body was shaking so violently that it exhausted me and I realised that if I let the cold affect me like this I wouldn't survive. So I started deep breathing exercises, using each exhalation to relax my muscles. The effect was immediate: my body relaxed and I even felt a sort of warmth spread over me.

Unfortunately, the sudden well-being didn't last. I was still cold. I started rocking back and forth, in the way that some mental patients do, whilst I continued my exercises. At the same time, I rubbed my frozen foot, my thighs and my arms. The variety of movements did me good, but the struggle against the cold was very hard. To cope, I just had to concentrate on what I was doing. And so the seconds, the minutes and the hours crept by during that interminable wait; my whole being fixed on one thing; to hold on, to hold on without setting a limit on how long for. I was determined to survive the cold, the fatigue and the pain. If Erik took an extra half hour, I would not let it get to me.

He arrived at last, apologising for having taken a few extra minutes to regain a bit of energy by drinking some hot coffee. All that mattered to me was that he was there, safe and sound; that was a sign that the nightmare would soon be over. When we got to the tent, all we would need to do was drink, eat, sleep, contact the people from Patriot Hills base, who had given us a lift up here and then sit back and wait for the plane, a Twin Otter, to come and get us. Unfortunately, things didn't quite turn out like that.

We had a good meal and a good rest, then Erik set off to fetch the radio we had left two hours' walk away. He returned a few hours later saying that he had tried in vain to contact the base at the agreed time; nine in the evening.

He added, but without any touch of panic in his voice, 'We'll try again tomorrow.'

It now became a priority to treat my wounds to prevent infection setting in. First of all the leg; having lost a fair bit of flesh and skin along the way the wound had become quite deep and wide. Erik cleaned it by squirting in large amounts of antiseptic, made a sterile dressing and surrounded it with a bit of foam rubber mat to try and keep the foot in line with the leg. He then repeated the operation on my elbow. The skin had been torn away over an area of ten centimetres long by five centimetres wide. Even though this wound looked almost as bad as the one on my leg, it didn't hurt. Unfortunately, as far as the shoulder and the foot were concerned, there was nothing we could do. He then gave me some antibiotics. We had no painkillers but I would not have taken them in any case; wanting to stay alert and aware of how I was doing. While we waited for the next radio session, we spent the time eating and sleeping.

Towards the middle of the afternoon, the wind got up and now Erik did start to worry. Would he be able to get the radio to work if there was a storm? It had a fifteen metre long aerial strung between two skis and this lifeline could be broken by heavy squalls. To our great relief, at around nine Erik did succeed in contacting Patriot Hills. Unlike most bases in Antarctica, this one is not a scientific research laboratory, but a sort of little airport set up by aviation enthusiasts for ferrying people and supplies, used right across this continent by 'adventurers' or 'explorers' of all kinds: walkers, tourists and climbers.

When I heard Erik outlining our situation over the radio and especially when he was giving our location co-ordinates from

11

the GPS I thought, 'We're saved.'

Now, even if the line broke, it wouldn't stop the rescuers from coming to fetch us. But actually we were not yet 'saved'. Towards 10pm the wind strengthened, preventing any aircraft from making an approach. It occurred to us that if the elements became any wilder, our tent would not be able to withstand it for long. Erik went outside to try and construct a snow break for our fragile shelter. He managed to build a little wall, about 30 centimetres high, all around us, before coming back inside, stiff with cold, and saying that if the conditions worsened, it would not be enough...

The wind battered the fabric, making such an awful din that there was no longer any chance of sleep. Lying on our backs, eyes wide open, we watched anxiously for the slightest weakness in the tent. After a few hours, light suddenly started to show through at a spot near the frame, where the fabric had been weakened by rubbing. Erik went out again. The wind was so violent that he couldn't stay upright on his knees, let alone stand. In other circumstances, seeing that great big guy sitting on the snow trying to rebuild our protective wall, might have been quite funny but I certainly had no inclination to laugh now. He soon gave up discouraged to come back into the shelter of the tent, hoping that the storm would abate soon and wondering if the tent would hold out for long enough.

Our anguish reached its height when, six hours later, the wind seemed to double its force. Two flexible tent poles folded under the force into sharp angles and, inevitably, the fabric around these folds started to wear away. To stop a rent forming, Erik held the fabric and spent the next hours with his arms up, holding the tent and being shaken by the attacking force of the wind. Staring fixedly at the altimeter, all I could do was hope for the storm to end. I was re-living the terrible wait at the bottom of the mountain face. Once again the only thing to do was to let time pass, but it was hard to bear and I felt my inner strength wearing away.

Twenty-four hours later, the rescue team was at last able to land and get us out of that hell. From the shocked and incredulous expressions of the people who met us at Patriot Hills, I could see that they saw me as someone who had come back from the dead. At last, under the care of a doctor I let myself go. I was helped by the morphine he gave me before trying to tend to my broken bone.

With my mind befuddled by the drugs and tears pouring down my cheeks for the first time since my fall, I understood what I had seen in their eyes and from half-overheard words in English, 'It's a miracle she survived... She's come back from hell...'

The story ended well. Today, thanks to a clever surgeon in Punta Arenas in Chile, I have no lasting effects from the accident.

Was it a miracle? That is not quite how I see it. Naturally one can never completely understand what allows someone to find the personal resources to face up to such a situation. However, what I am absolutely sure of, is that I would never have made it back without the accumulation of climbing experience dating right back to the first time I set foot on the rocks.

A PASSION IS BORN

A man without a landscape is destitute.
Patrick Modiano

WHEN I was a child, my parents used to take their offspring out at the weekends to get some fresh air in the forest of Fontainebleau, where my father went climbing with friends. At the time, there were four of us – all girls and I am the eldest. We had no interest in climbing and preferred wild games of hide and seek among the rocks. Having spent the whole day chasing each other around, we were taken home exhausted which, as far as our parents were concerned, was one of the objects of the exercise because we were quite a handful. As the years went on, there were fewer excursions to the forest. The family grew – a boy and then another girl – and any outings became major expeditions. I think our parents' keenness fizzled out since the result of our well-balanced education was to make us less and less biddable...

Around the age of eleven I mostly stayed at home, in Savigny-sur-Orge in the Parisian suburbs. I had lots of friends with whom I played outdoors all weekend: roller skating, riding our bikes, ball games, marbles... and actually it was almost as much fun as going to the forest. That continued up until the time when the games lost their joyous spontaneity. My friends, both girls and boys, lost interest in outdoor games; preferring instead to gossip, listen to music and to stay shut indoors for entire afternoons. Alternatively, we would hang around the town 'getting up to no good', as the adults called it. For the most part we didn't do anything really bad; the worst being to smoke cigarettes in secret… but I was badly behaved, irritable and at a loose end, not knowing how to fill my time.

My parents worried about me and suggested I might like to join the French Alpine Club to do some climbing. I jumped at the suggestion. I had dreamed of doing that ever since I had overheard a friend of my mother's telling my parents about it. I knew that climbing could lead to mountaineering, in other words being in the mountains, and that fitted in perfectly with the first thing I ever wanted to do when I was grown up – to be a shepherdess.

In the September of the year that I was twelve, I was duly enrolled at the CAF (Club Alpin Français) which meant that I was free to go to the forest of Fontainebleau every Sunday. The day began at five in the morning as I had to get into Paris to the Gare de Lyon station; from there I took the 8:23 train along with all the other club members; the 'cafistes'. Yes. You certainly needed to be keen and those who were less so soon dropped out. I looked forward to the outing so much that I started preparing on Wednesdays to be absolutely sure that everything I needed would be ready. There was no question of me wearing anything other than my favourite worn green velvet jeans, my green sweater (in the same state) and my splendid orange and green checked shirt. It was essential that these were all ready in advance; washed and softened in the tumble dryer.

Green was my favourite colour, although it was also the colour I had been given by my mother. With the arrival of a son and then a daughter expanding the family, she had the idea of a colour coded system for each of her six children, to avoid them squabbling over possessions. That was how I got the green pullover knitted by Grandma, the green school satchel, green socks, green towel… and in my eyes they went beautifully together. I especially liked the colour which I thought let me blend in with the natural background of the forest. All that remained as a finishing touch to my preparations, was to put my climbing boots and socks neatly in the bottom of my rucksack, to which a picnic would be added at the last moment. I was completely mortified if this ritual was not followed to the letter.

I had no difficulty getting up on Sundays, despite the early hour. I enjoyed making up for the minimal breakfast at home by scoffing hot croissants and baguettes bought from the nearest open bakery, and I loved the solitary walk through a still-sleeping Savigny, eagerly anticipating the joys to come. The first few times I was quite overcome and I must say rather proud to be going into Paris all on my own. And when I got there, the streets were completely deserted. I was terrified of being late; of being unable to find the right platform or not being able to recognise the right group of people. But of course it was always fine and the train took about twenty of us to Bois-le-Roi from whence we had a ten kilometre hike to reach the rocks. But this was far from being a chore, on the contrary, I appreciated the sounds, sights and smells of the forest.

As we walked along, I listened with fascination to the others' chatting about the summer they had just spent in the mountains, some talked discretely, others described their exploits in lurid detail. I felt a bit lost, even foreign, amongst all these strangers and, as I had just spent the last two months at the seaside, felt the last thing they would want to hear was my tales of going fishing. I was thrilled and fascinated by the special climbers' vocabulary, though that isolated me even more, as the sport of climbing has its own language and climbers forming a micro-society need to be initiated into its rites and codes. I had everything to learn.

It wasn't until the first club outing to Barbizon, the Apremont Gorges to be precise, that I really approached the forest from the climber's point of view. Once all the juniors had been rounded up and given a few moments to recharge their batteries, everyone was divided into little groups spread around the rocks. The boulders were marked with different coloured arrows which, as I soon learned, corresponded to different levels of difficulty. I had been put with a group of ten or so teenagers who were to start with a yellow route. We were to take it in turns to try; I listened with feverish attention as the instructor gave advice to the others until it was my turn at last. Slightly overwhelmed by the feeling that all eyes were now on me, I took off and, surprise, surprise, got up all the boulders at first try; amazed not to have found the route difficult even if it was for beginners.

After doing about a dozen boulders I started to fidget; I was raring to go and had had enough of waiting. In the end I couldn't stand it anymore and wandered off to explore other boulders nearby but not on our climb, which earned me a good telling off. The instructor was right of course. It could have been dangerous and he was responsible for my safety but that was not the way I saw it and I was very cross.

Fortunately another instructor, who had not been busy up to then, stepped in to take charge of me. Now I was allowed to try as much as I wanted. I had a few goes, made a few mistakes and then up I went. I got up everything and was thoroughly proud of myself. Inside I was jubilant, feeling that I was making incredibly fast progress, carefully memorising each step and each move to be able to reuse them later. There was a jumble of thoughts inside my head, and I felt as if I were on the brink of a new world.

Going back to the group, which was already looking at me differently, I saw my first instructor going for the circuits I had just been on. It could be that he didn't know them, or was unable to judge their difficulty straight away, but he failed to get up one of them. I do believe that on that day, my new climbing friends almost worshipped me.

My relationship with that instructor being now somewhat strained, I was in seventh heaven when his colleague – who had given me the precious gift of letting me discover myself – suggested he show me some other climbs. At first I was a bit embarrassed to accept but I could soon tell that he was having as much fun as I was.

From then on that was how we met up every weekend to tackle circuits, one after another, until it was time to go home. Climbing had to stop by the middle of the afternoon so as not to miss the evening train. I used to get home about nine in the evening with scraped fingers, utterly exhausted but happy with my day. Over dinner I told my family all about it, but none of them could truly appreciate how much it meant to me and over time I talked less and less; just coming out with a laconic 'that was fine,' or 'that didn't work,' depending on the day or the climb. Actually there was not much point even in saying anything at all, as one glance at my face as I came through the front door was information enough.

On Monday mornings I would be crippled by my aching muscles; barely able to walk along a pavement and it always took me two or three days to recover. The rest of the week would drag by waiting for another Sunday to finally arrive. My initiation came as a real revelation to me and I was completely hooked on climbing; thinking about it in the daytime and dreaming about it at night.

When I got a club newsletter, I read it from cover to cover – births, marriages and deaths included – and piously kept it next to my bed where, before going to sleep, I would re-read it, immerse myself in it and daydream about the program of trips which was a promise of glories to come. I would not have missed a single outing even though in winter the conditions were much tougher, with shorter days, frequent rain and it could be very cold. It was sometimes even snowy when I went climbing and the holds needed to be cleared; a sure way to numb fingers.

Having heard that the best of the group would be chosen to go on a summer course in the mountains, I tested my fitness and got to know my abilities and my physical and mental limits. In anticipation of the course, I worked furiously, always doing more and by so doing asserted myself both in my own eyes and to others. I was always anxious to do things correctly, so if I was told, 'In the mountains, stubbing your feet against a stone could be fatal,' I took great care to step over things with big, smooth movements, or if they said, 'You need to be strong,' I showed how well I could walk, that I wasn't bothered by the cold and that I could take anything in my stride without it altering my good mood.

One day, as an endurance test, I even went so far as to climb all day in the snow wearing shorts. Indeed I think that I felt the need to do far more than the others because, as the youngest in the group, I didn't want to be seen as a weakling. One day, seeing how awful the weather was, my parents took pity on me and had the misguided idea of coming to fetch me. They were only trying to be kind, but I was furious. I was with the others and wanted to be like the others not be mollycoddled. In any case I rather enjoyed the relaxation of walking after the effort of climbing. I found the return journey calming; a time when I could clear my head and, like an automaton, allow my exhausted but happy body to carry me along.

The first outing to the cliffs took place during the Easter holidays. What a thrill! In my twelve year old eyes going up cliffs seemed to be the start of some really serious climbing and I was wide-eyed with admiration for anyone who did it. It still held all its mystery for me and I could barely imagine what it would be like. For the occasion, my parents bought me my own harness and an orange locking karabiner. I was even going to be allowed to use my father's sleeping bag. Just two things upset me: because I still hadn't grown much at the time, the harness was a children's one, and I thought its bright colours of red and orange clashed.

I will forever remember that first outing to Saffres, in the Côte-d'Or, where I climbed for the first time using rope and karabiners the way mountaineers did in the photographs I pored over. Actually, when I got to the foot of the cliff, I was a bit disappointed at first, I was expecting it to have been at least as high as my apartment block, though in fact it was 30 to 35 metres high, which was the equivalent of twelve floors. I had just been fooled by the false perspective given by the long vertical lines on modern buildings.

We started off by climbing L'éclair, which got its name (lightening) from a long gash which has to be followed to reach the top. In terms of the complexity of the climb, it rated second on a scale of one to six from the easiest to the most difficult. Later, as climbers progressed, a level seven was added in 1977, eight in 1982 and since 1990 there has even been a grade nine. I wasn't quite up to those levels at the time.

The task fell to me to belay the lead climber, an instructor. He showed me how to do it and he tied the knot for my own rope. At last I was roped up just like a proper, great mountaineer. I tried very hard to emulate the way I had seen belaying done by watching at Fontainebleau and by looking in books and magazines. Flattered as I was by the trust put in me, I was also a bit worried. Would I manage? Would I, small as I was, be able to hold that big, beefy guy if he foolishly took it into his head to fall? I tried to take comfort from the thought that he must know what he was doing. When he reached the top of the cliff, he called that it was my turn.

That was the green light I had been waiting for, and I was off like a rocket. Even though I have told myself time and again that I have all the time in the world, I don't know why, but I have always climbed at top speed. It might be so as not to hold up my climbing companions or just due to a naturally impatient nature. Nowadays I have learned to breathe through the effort, in those early days I got to the top of the routes quite out of breath. I was however aware that I had certain talents – it was then that I discovered that I had a good head for heights.

One thing continued to dog me: as I was rushing, every time I got to a piton, I forgot to unclip and continued past... only to find myself pulled up short with a jerk 50 centimetres higher, wondering what had happened and cursing the bastard who had stopped me from... oh good grief! Of course! I had yet again forgotten to free the rope. Each time I was absolutely furious with myself.

I did another two routes of the same level that morning at Saffres, taking great pride in not heaving on any pitons, or needing the leader either to hold me or, worse still to have to pull me up.

In the afternoon, it was I who led. Before setting off, I scanned the cliff meticulously, experiencing for the first time both the pleasure of leading a pitch with just a glance to iden-tify potential difficulties and holds, and also that shiver of ex-citement when the body is ready for action and ready to defy the void. Once I was up and away, I moved smoothly with perfect co-ordination, my muscles responding to all that was asked of them. I managed to get to the top as leader. For the first time in my life, I felt complete.

That scrupulous observation from the bottom of the cliff has become the way I have always done things since. It is a reflex I have each time I set off and it stands me in good stead. I got in another two climbs on other, slightly harder routes and the harder it got, the more I enjoyed it. I loved the stealthy race of hand and eye over the stone in search of the right bump which, when found at last, became the hold to enable the fol-lowing thrill of a powerful lift. I took great satisfaction from feeling my muscles and tendons working as I went from hold to hold.

Climbing gave me a sensation of well-being. Far from it hindering me, I felt that my body was full of unlimited re-serves. I had already proved this to myself at Fontainebleau after tackling several climbs one after the other. I was com-pletely serene and had perfect concentration as I took those routes that day. The more I climbed, the more I wanted to; climbing was gradually taking me over. It was like a drug to which I was becoming addicted.

The summer holidays were getting close. I was the youngest of the ten beginners chosen to take the course in the mountains, where we were to spend three weeks in Valgaude-mar, I was completely over-excited at the thought of camping like shepherds and of getting so high that I would be nearer to the God in whom I still believed. I had been given a strict, religious education which, even though I was less blinkered than I had been, thanks to a dawning awareness of hypocrisy in what some believers told me, still had its hold.

My parents kitted me out from head to toe. They bought me a new rucksack. It was huge and blue and there were so many pockets on it that it took me ages to find anything I had stashed away. I must say that it was not actually ideal for climbing in the mountains, as the pockets kept catching on things and its weight unbalanced me, but none of that mattered as it really looked the part. This was the first time I had been away from my parents for such a long time and, despite my delight at going to the mountains, I was a little apprehensive about being homesick. Previously, after I had been away from the bosom of my family for more than a few days, there had been floods of tears but this time nothing at all; I was floating on a little cloud. Fortunately for my self esteem, being among people who were certainly no longer affected by insecurities like that, meant there was no way I was going to be such a baby.

We were looked after by a guide and several instructors and just spent the first two days learning to coil ropes, handling them and tying knots. It wasn't thrilling but I behaved myself. Next stage, the climbing school was better but not yet what I was after, though I did have the satisfaction of getting our guide into a tight spot. We had found some boulders which were right for us and were trying out some circuits when, after a few goes, I found a rather hard one. The guide took quite a while, struggling to get up it and was in a foul temper and swearing about having been shown up by a little kid. To get his own back and to save face, he went off and found a big overhang, rather boastfully, I got round that too.

Next, we went up to a mountain refuge for the first time. We had to carry our food rations with us, dividing them up equally between ourselves. These consisted mostly of tins of food some of which weighed five kilos. A few of the others balked at carrying these big loads, on the pretext that their bags were too small but I, so very proud of my enormous backpack, offered to take some off them. As we walked up the mountain, we had been told to go at the same pace and to stop from time to time for a drink. I had fallen into second place, just behind the guide and was following briskly in his footsteps so that when he paused to tie a bootlace, he told me just to carry on at the front of the group. I was enjoying the scenery so much and, in my eagerness to see the refuge, I speeded up without realising what I was doing. The team became more and more strung out and soon only one of the cadets was behind me. We were happy to go along at our own pace and definitely less bothered than the rest, who kept having to wait for each other.

We got to the refuge well before the others but while they were trailing up far behind us, they seemed to have spent most of their time planning the rocket we would get when they finally caught up with us. We 'shouldn't have charged off like that, should have waited for the instructors...' and so on and so forth. As for the guide, he was bathed in sweat and seemed somewhat peeved at not having been able to keep up.

I was amazed at how comfortable the refuge was, with its gas cooker, fully equipped kitchen, crockery and cutlery. We settled in, cooking a meal and organising who was sleeping where. The guide, who had now noticed me and was intrigued by me, came and took the bunk next to mine. Never having slept in a refuge before, I wasn't quite sure what to do, so I copied everything he did: unfolding my blanket, rolling up clothes to make a pillow and then putting my torch carefully within reach. He spread his T-shirt out to dry but unfortunately mine was already dry. I slept very well but at three o'clock in the morning, time for action. The guide got up and went outside. I crept after him. He was peeing whilst looking up at the sky. 'It's going to be fine all day' he exclaimed and seemed pleased.

He came back in just as I was pulling the blanket back up over my nose. Had he made any other weather prediction, I think I would have burst into tears, I was so desperate to climb a mountain. Just like him, I had got my things prepared the night before and was ready in no time and happy to help him get breakfast together while the others took their time getting up. He started to get annoyed; telling them to get a move on and, seeing the state he was working himself into, I started to worry that it would be too late to set off.

At long last, the group left the refuge and by dawn we reached the snowline. The guide stopped and told us to put on our crampons. This was another first for me but I was prepared; having practised how to do it, I got mine on almost as quickly as he did. All around us it was chaos. Some had forgotten to adjust their crampons, others couldn't get the straps right… and this madness went on for a whole hour. The guide told them impatiently that if they didn't manage to walk better, there would be no point in continuing that day. I was champing at the bit to get on but said nothing. Just as he was speaking, one of the girls fell and slid away on the snow. Things really did seem to have got off to a bad start.

The group eventually muddled up a 100 metres of névé, to be told by the guide that we would spend the day practising on the snow and that the high slopes could wait for another time. My disappointment did not last long as we actually had a lot of fun. We had to make each other fall over and support each other by making teams with ropes; one instructor to two learners. Somehow, by a stroke of 'luck', I managed to find myself paired up with the good-looking guide. I was in seventh heaven. Whilst he pretended to fall, I was supposed to hold him and he was properly throwing himself into it. It really isn't easy to hold someone on a snowy slope and I needed to brace myself in readiness before he even fell, so I wondered how I would manage in the case of a sudden and unexpected tumble. The next exercise involved diving head first down the slope and then getting back upright as quickly as possible and we had great fun messing around in the snow. The day without climbing turned out not so bad after all.

The next day we finally got down to some serious stuff: we went to the Pic du Loup, taking in the Col du Loup on the way. To reach the Pic involved a straightforward hike in the snow without a single crevasse to cross and no hint of danger, however hard I tried to imagine it. Then I was thoroughly unimpressed with the climb, not understanding how to use the rope, except to hinder or to tangle oneself up in. What was more, the leader to whom I was roped, was so nervous on the ridge, that he wouldn't get up off all fours. The guide looked round from time to time, roaring with laughter to see how we were getting on, whilst I was fuming.

As each day passed, I became increasingly intolerant. I felt as if I were just waiting around the whole time, and my friends' mistakes and their anxiety irritated me. I attracted a succession of critical remarks about my so-called 'unruly' behaviour and if I was told off, it was because I was not willing to learn at the same pace as the others, to limit my pace on the walks, to stay on the paths...

One morning, just as we were about to go up to a refuge, I awoke feeling really out of sorts with a headache and a raging sore throat. There was no way I was prepared to miss what might turn out to be a climb, and so I said nothing, hoping that the walk would pep me up. But once I had struggled up to the refuge and put my bag down... I fainted. There was no longer any question of me prancing about and the others were all in a state of panic. I was put to bed and kept my friends awake all night with my feverish moaning. I had no say in the matter; the others would go off for their climb and I would wait in for them under a heap of blankets. I did have some consolation however, as the guide stayed behind with me. Though when he wanted me to be taken off the mountain by helicopter, I found the strength to protest that I wasn't ill and could perfectly well walk back rather than the shame of a helicopter... though I did have to give in on one count; he would carry my bag down for me. There was no way of getting out of a visit to the doctor's, resulting in a boring course of antibiotics and a period of bed rest and hot drinks rendered delightful by being waited upon hand and foot by my protector, the guide Roland. He promised to take me on a climb which would be much more impressive with more beautiful scenery than the one I had just missed

After the three prescribed rest days, I was at last able to go off again with the others. Roland had to leave us, to be replaced by another bad-tempered guide, who wanted everything his way, ignored the wishes of the group leaders and did everything at a mad speed. Without any sensitivity towards those around him, he messed up the supplies by changing menus and shocked the young ladies by sleeping naked in the communal dormitory.

When the course came to an end, my parents gave in at last to my pestering to allow me to stay on and do some proper stuff; that is to say do the route which Roland had promised, namely the north face of Sirac, the highest point in the Valgaudemar range. At last I was truly experiencing the mountains, the joy of pulling oneself up with silence all around and the pleasure of reaching the top. We were climbing like real mountaineers with just one team, alternating leads. When there were fifteen of us, the mountains had not lived up to my expectations. Then Roland offered to take me along with him on climbs with his clients and in the space of a few days, I gained far more experience than I had throughout the course.

This life lasted until my pocket money ran out, as I had to pay for the hostel and food, so to stay on I offered to do cleaning in the refuges and to pick Genepi, a little flower growing wild in the mountains from which an alcoholic drink of the same name is distilled. I had noticed some splendid, but somewhat inaccessible plants which, with a bit of an effort allowed me to pick huge quantities. But oh dear! Getting them back down was a drama. The ground rolled away around me and everything I tried to catch hold of to steady myself came off in my hands. The stones were just in soil and slid away under my feet. The tiniest rolling pebble set off a real little avalanche and all was shifting about me. The foot of the mountain was just a huge mound of scree. I was just like the silly little girl of the old cartoons *Bécassine*, stuck up a mountain and scared to death.

For a whole hour, I stayed on hands and knees not daring to move, unable to go backwards or forwards. I thought of what my parents would say if they knew what a fix I had got myself into. In the end, I managed to get a grip on myself by talking to out loud. 'Come on Catherine, calm down, easy does it! Even if it takes two days you'll manage, left foot there, well done. Now tap your right foot on that stone to see if it'll hold' and mostly it didn't hold. It was awful, as soon as I took a hesitant step, I imagined myself rolling down and smashing to smithereens at the bottom. My life flashed past me in my head: parents, brother, sisters 'all gone forever.' Each second was a stay of execution. 'Come on Catherine, you are scared stiff, pull yourself together.' I gave myself a talking to and es- caped, step by step, after three hours.

I had ventured off into a place where no rescuers would have found me and my voice was still shaking as I told my tale that evening. To this day I can still remember that the tinned fruit salad I ate to calm myself down tasted like resurrection.

The extra time I had been granted by my parents was com- ing to an end as were the school holidays. After a summer like that, I was in no mood to be back in a classroom. All I could think of was going back to the mountains. Roland had sug- gested I spend a few weekends climbing with him and I could see that they would need to be carefully planned around my schoolwork, to have the time off. I was not optimistic when I told my parents and got the anticipated reaction, 'Don't even think of it. Come on darling, it would be much too tiring for you to spend weekends in the mountains... Anyway what about your homework? And we don't even know this guide.' And so, as I expected, I had to dispense with their permission.

The fear of not so very long ago of crying when separated from my parents was a thing of the past. I elaborated an intricate scenario: officially I would be spending weekends in the forest of Fontainebleau with the Alpine Club cadets; actually, I would be meeting my teacher/guide/friend near Gap in the foothills of the Alps. I would be setting off from the same place, the Gare de Lyon in Paris, but for a much longer overnight train journey, and more significantly a much more expensive one. To eke out my very meagre resources, I devised some devious schemes: I got one reduced price ticket at the family rate, valid for two months, at departure and then played a game of hide and seek with the ticket inspector (to avoid him I hid under seats or, much more comfortable, in the overhead luggage nets). On arrival I found an alternative exit by sneaking amongst the goods trains.

When my ticket expired, I went and got a refund, saying that it had not been used, bought another one and did the same thing all over again. Thus I was able to climb without hindrance in the Vercors, on Mont Aiguille, at Archiane, at Glandasse among other mountains. Although I had often done two climbs in a weekend, I could not betray myself on Sunday evenings by seeming too tired. It was exciting but I was a little ill at ease. What if my parents found out what I was up to? To stack the odds in my favour and carry on going 'like a good girl to Fontainebleau' which my parents were wholly in favour of – I needed to play the part of the hard-working schoolgirl on weekdays. My marks went up as a result and everyone was happy.

Having got this stratagem down to a tee, I took the liberty of enjoying a little cross-country skiing in the springtime – unwise move. I got home much too tanned and nearly blind; I had skied without goggles and was slightly snow-blind. Try passing that off as a weekend just south of Paris. I spun them a yarn about sand blowing in my eyes and my poor father trawled around on a Sunday evening trying to buy eye drops. My heart was in my mouth. In the event it was all so dramatic that they didn't examine my version of the events too closely. Nevertheless their suspicions were aroused and they said that the following weekend someone had to come and fetch me from home. How to get round this one? I talked to a school friend with an older brother; I needed an accomplice, could he play the part? He agreed but, to my great surprise, turned up carrying a motorcycle helmet. That did not do the trick, as I was supposed to be collected by car, and my mother started having doubts again. I made up some far-fetched explanation and succeeded, *in extremis*, in getting out of the house. I was thrilled to be riding on the back of a motorbike for the first time in my life. He dropped me at the station in Juvisy, from where I hopped on the first Paris-bound train, reaching the Gare de Lyon two hours early.

Reluctant to leave my bag in the train, I decided instead to settle down to wait for the departure time on an elevated luggage trolley. I had fun watching the passersby, observing their comings and goings, what they were wearing and carrying, their expressions when suddenly, horror of horrors! I saw my father coming towards the platform. His face was dark with anger and I was literally petrified on my trolley, heart beating fast and unable to think. It took me a few seconds to react and in total panic I leapt off my perch and dived under a mail train, praying that no one would pull me out or, worse still that the train wouldn't leave. Crouching low, I could see my father as he paced the platform, eyes searching, jaw jutting and with an increasingly livid expression. When he checked inside all the compartments, I thought what a stroke of luck it was that I had not left my bag lying around. He even carried on looking for me after the train had left and did not leave until after the last departure for Briançon; he wasn't born yesterday.

To be safe, I hid until one in the morning, huddled up, waiting for the station to be empty. Only then, creeping like a fugitive, did I dare to come out of my hiding place, carefully checking by the ticket counters and then round each of the newspaper stands and bars – no lurking father. I had avoided the worst, which would have been to come face to face with him. I knew what he was like when he was angry. There was by now no point in leaving for Gap and even less in going home so I tried to phone my godfather, but in vain.

Where could I go to spend the night? I hung around the station nervously until two o'clock trying to adjust my features into a waiting-for-a-train expression. But there were hardly any trains left at that time of night. It was at that point that an African man approached me kindly, asking what I was doing. He told me that the staff would soon be clearing the station for the night and 'in any case it's not sensible for you to be here.' I rather thought he was right. Then he offered to let me go home with him, where I would be safe. He was a stranger, but I certainly didn't want to be taken off to a police station either.

At first I did not reply, but he persuaded me by saying that he was a teacher and if I did not trust him, he could take me to a youth centre instead. That reassured me. After all, he was quite nice and I decided to follow him home. As he lived on the outskirts of Paris, I found myself in a train, telling my woes to a man who was willing to listen. What a relief that was after all that had happened. At his place, he gave me some cereal from his country to eat, which I had not tried before – it was good – and put on some African music which made me feel totally disorientated. When we went to bed, he asked if I wanted his bed or somewhere else. I opted to sleep on the floor as I often did to get into training for bivouacking, and at home I was even toughening myself up on the balcony.

I talked on and on to that man, almost all night, only going to sleep in the small hours. Never before had I confided in anyone so much. When I awoke, I was alone with a note next to me saying that I could stay several days if it suited me to do so but if I wanted to leave, I should just pull the door shut behind me. It was really an unbelievable stroke of luck to have come upon such a good person. He had not tried to touch a single hair on my head. I thought I had better go to Fontainebleau for three or four days just as I had told my parents and that is where I was just a few hours later.

My spirits were as low as the moss under my feet, I was

weighed down with misery and feeling thoroughly listless. What was more, my rucksack was much too heavy. It was a steamy hot day and I had not a drop to drink in the blasted bag. My grumpy thoughts beat in time with my walk from Bois-le-Roi to Barbizon; I was fed up with a life in which I was not allowed to go to the mountains. No one understood me, no one loved me, I had hardly any help...

At Barbizon I bought a bottle of water and a packet of biscuits and headed for the Apremont Gorge for some bouldering. My dark mood lifted, my problems forgotten, my mind cleared completely as climbing wrought its miraculous effect on me. I was absorbed by my sensations, feeling indefatigable with a perfect flow of moves.

Throughout the day I came across a few climbers with the same determination as me but towards the end of the afternoon, I was alone once more. I had not taken any notice of the rather strange behaviour of two men until, after a while I was worried to find them really closing in on me. I was much too small to contemplate taking them on all by myself. How could I get hold of my bag, which I had left hidden under the rock where I had intended to sleep? I did not like this situation at all; there was nobody around and I had no way of escaping. Trying to run with my big bag was out of the question. Should I try to hide in the bushes, perhaps playing hide and seek all night, jumping at the slightest sound? Good ideas can be born of necessity: why not take refuge on top of a rock which those clumsy oafs could not climb? I needed a nice, comfortable boulder without any other easy access and number one on the red circuit suited the bill perfectly. It is very high and those two slobs with their fat stomachs could never reach me.

I collected my stuff and charged at top speed to the providential boulder. I couldn't believe how fast I managed to go despite the weight of my bag. With diabolical strength I climbed up to my safe haven – just in time as the two geezers had broken into a run. Somewhat vexed, they started sweet talking me and asking what I was afraid of. With as much composure as I could muster, I calmly replied 'animals'. We were now acting out the fable of the fox and the crow, but I knew the story and I was not going to be had.

They started with seemingly kind words, 'You are very sweet and we would like to take you out to dinner.' I watched them from my perch, munching my biscuits and wondering when they would start to have a go. This was going to be fun. And here it came, 'Oh well, as you don't want to come and be with us, we'll just come up to keep you company.' I was fairly sure they would not make it, but watching one of them give his mate a leg up, I started to worry I had been too optimistic.

Those pigs disgusted me but all I could do was show bravado. I laughed at them and made fun of them which succeeded in making them lose what strength they actually had. Reassured at last, after a few minutes I was able to laugh properly at the comical scene of two ridiculous, overweight slime-bags dressed in city clothes stuck on the ground. Angry now, they altered their tone and threatened nasty things.

The star turn of the show was when they got undressed. I pretended not to notice them prancing about in the nude at the foot of the boulder and feigned sleep in the hope they would calm down, but being ignored made no difference and I was treated to a masterly lesson in sex education. I was spared no technical term or vulgarity. At just thirteen years old, in that one night I learned more on the subject than most children of my age. Unable to sleep, I was tensed in readiness to crush the two sex maniacs' fingers, should they make it up onto my rock. I watched their every move and ended up worrying when they fell silent. They did not give up until daybreak, but I waited until a few climbers were around before daring to come down.

I still had another three days to spend in the forest but had not the heart to climb, so I went and hung around in Barbizon and bought some food to improve my mood. That was worse than anything. I did not know anyone, thought the people there unfriendly and found myself being followed again as I went back to the forest. From the look of him he was just a labourer who worked in the vicinity and fortunately he soon turned off my path to get to his site. It was the last straw and I just could not be there alone any longer. All I could do now was to find a safe bolt hole. I held out for 48 hours, ending up going home a day earlier than expected. My parents seemed pleased to have me home. They did not quite understand these trips but as they wanted to be liberal and were pleased to see me growing up independent and they did not delve too deeply into what I was up to. It was not until ten years later that I told them what really happened during those times when I was away from the bosom of my family.

I did not feel like telling any more lies after that especially memorable episode. Climbing with a heavy conscience spoilt my enjoyment and so there were no more weekends in the mountains. I would be there soon anyway, as the summer holidays were approaching and most years my parents rented a chalet for us all. This year it would be in the Queyras near the Italian border where, despite the lack of climbing, we would be able to go for long walks in the Alpine meadows, enjoying the greenery, the flowers, the cows and the little streams which I have always so adored.

As we were driving down the motorway, I suddenly hit on the idea of going round the Oisans on my own. My parents were all for it; especially my father who immediately offered to take me there, leave me at the starting point of my itinerary and fetch me again ten days later. I could hardly believe my ears. How many parents would be willing to let their fourteen year old daughter go for a long hike alone in the mountains? I was very grateful to them for their trust in me.

A week later I set off from the village of La Grave. Having decided that I would be completely autonomous, my rucksack contained tent, sleeping bag, clothes, food for several days etc. For the first few days it was really tough. How heavy my bag was. What could have possessed me not to want to sleep in mountain huts? But I stuck with my decision for the whole trip.

Actually, all the way round, I never once felt alone. Large

numbers of walkers take that route round the Oisans forest and they frequently talked to me, surprised to see me on my own. I sometimes even spent an entire day walking with the same people. Ten days later I was back at La Grave to rendezvous with my father.

When the holidays were over I went back to the routine of my weekends in Fontainebleau. The hills the other cadets wanted to climb no longer held any attraction for me, so I used to head off alone on Sundays. The routine was as follows: Gare de Lyon 08:23 train, a ten to fifteen kilometres brisk walk and then I was on my beloved rocks. By now I knew the forest, with its innumerable paths and secret places, like the back of my hand. I saw stags and does and one day I even found myself nose to nose with a sounder of wild boar who were crossing my path. In a twinkling, before I could even smack my lips, the group had gone on their way, taking not the slightest notice of me.

I chose my climbing spots according to the weather. When it is wet, some places are drier than others; when hot, it is better to seek shade. Around the rocks it is unusual to be alone for long. Sometimes I found myself at the foot of a climb with another solo climber who would give me advice and we would end up doing some of a circuit together and then, at the end of the day, arrange to meet up again the following weekend. That way, I met several 'Bleausards', the Fotainebleau specialists. Ultimately the world of climbers is very small and we all knew each other more or less, at least by sight. As time went on, I was offered lifts on the Sundays and soon I no longer needed to catch the train.

One of these friends, Pierre Richard, who was especially kind to me, showed incredible patience. I had first met him in the Cuvier, the area which is a dead cert for meeting climbers, as that is where the most difficult climbs are to be found. These rocks all have a name and a history, their routes having been pioneered by such greats as Pierre Allain or Robert

Paragot. The climbers of the Club Alpin Français spoke of them in hushed tones, perpetuating the myth that these most terrible of cliffs were only suitable for the very best of climbers to attempt. One day, I decided to try them out anyway. Creeping like a mouse, I slid unobtrusively between the rocks to look at the amazing boulders with their amazing climbers.

I was very curious to watch the comings and goings of these 'greats' of rock climbing. Some of them were small, some very tall but what they all had in common was that they were slim, or not to put too fine a point on it, skinny. I thought to myself that I had got off to a bad start. If I wanted one day to be their equal, I would need to do something about changing my build. After a while, I stood casually in front of climb one on the blue circuit, carefully observing the way the climbers were getting up it. When at last I found myself alone, I hastily pulled on my climbing boots and had a try. After a few attempts, I had climbed it. Emboldened by my success, I tried number two. This was considerably more gymnastic and I was nearly at the top when I fell off... 'Better luck next time.'

I did no better on the next few climbs but while I was struggling away on number seven, a big, blond guy came up to the rock to take the same route. That was Pierre. He was taking the blue circuit at a run. When he saw how upset I was, he showed me how to go about it and then, with great kindness, explained the moves I should do and how to take advantage of the few holds there were. I was ashamed because, despite his help, I still couldn't do it. Whether through lack of strength or technique, or a combination of the two, I was missing something, but I didn't know what. Whatever it was, I was completely stumped by all the climbs he showed me and, if I had been alone, would have burst into tears of rage.

Technique in rock climbing is very important as compensation for lack of strength. Pierre taught me how to position myself in relation to the rock, how to use the outside edges of my feet on the holds, to take handholds facing each other and reversed, how to jam my fists into cracks, etc. By the end of the

35

day, I was exhausted. We arranged to meet again at the same place the following weekend.

I went home delighted, but did not want my parents to know. I was going through a dreadful adolescent phase that year and was utterly intolerant of anything they said to me. At school, I kept my grades up in maths, English, Russian, Latin... basically all that was needed to keep me in the highest set with the biggest cows for teachers.

I felt as if I were living a parallel life. All my climbing friends were eight or ten years older than me and with the teenagers back at school, who talked of nothing but parties, petty squabbles and their teenage complexes, I assumed the rather unusual role of confidante. They all came to me with their little crises and their huge problems. My role was to offer reassurance and encouragement as best I could. But I too had things in my life which bothered me, yet no one in whom I could confide. To my climbing chums, I was just 'the little kid who climbs well,' and no more.

For a whole year I was moody and miserable, with only one distraction: my flute, which I played every day. That too created a barrier between me and the other students, who only liked pop music and the latest hits, while I only listened to and played classical music. I was in the orchestra of the Savigny music college. Rehearsals were twice a week and I went along eagerly, sometimes even entertaining dreams of becoming a flautist. I had started to learn the flute when I was eight years old, because at that age I was convinced that a real shepherdess would need to be able to play one. Actually I dreamed of playing the recorder, but the music college only taught the flute so I had to compromise.

After a year of rock climbing, I had a nagging problem: I had put on ten kilos. It had happened gradually but the ever-tightening waistband of my jeans was a sure sign. However much I resolved to eat less, every time I went past a baker's I could not help buying myself a cake or sweets. Even twenty metres before, my conscience was telling me not to give in this time, to walk past as if I hadn't noticed but I was irresistibly drawn into the den of iniquity. Anyway, I always carried sweets around with me which I munched incessantly, one after the other, until they were all gone.

After school, I prepared gargantuan snacks for myself. One of my favourite recipes involved melting a bar of chocolate in a mug of hot milk to make a lovely, creamy goo. Then I carefully cut a stick of French bread in two, spread it with butter and dipped it in, bit by bit, voluptuously until I was totally replete. I refused to settle down to my homework until after this little pick-me-up. With my bursting stomach and mind dulled as I digested, I did sometimes have difficulty concentrating. Then at dinner time, I stuck to my principles and decided to be on a diet, telling my parents, 'I'm not having any dinner this evening,' they did not argue. Around ten, I would start to feel a little peckish and half an hour later would pounce on the left-overs, puddings if possible...

Periodically, I would take myself in hand and start a strict diet; usually on a Monday. For breakfast: only tea; for lunch: a boiled egg and an apple; dinner: soup and another apple. Same again the next day, except that in the evening I gave in, exhausted from hunger and the effort of resisting temptation. On the Wednesday, to make up for last night's broken diet, I would go running around the streets of Savigny, dressed like an onion in as many layers as possible to make me sweat. When I got home and weighed myself, I would have lost a kilo. In celebration of this success, I allowed myself a little more food on Thursday and then on Friday I went mad; really letting the diet go because at the weekend I knew I would lose all those ugly, extra kilos...

I actually would have lost a kilo or two by the weekend, only to put the weight back on, before falling into the same vicious cycle which did me no good: either for my morale or my training. To climb well, you need to be light. There was however something I could do: fitness training at home. Every evening I forced myself to do half an hour of abdominal exercises, having noticed that I could not lift my legs very high for overhangs and that my thighs felt heavy. After those exercises, I lay down on the floor under my desk chair, held its edges and did sets of ten pull-ups. I did have a barbell, but at first I could not lift it more than three times and so went back to my under-chair position.

Then I thought of doing press-ups – useful at the very top of boulders. I even went so far as to make myself a sauna. I ran boiling hot water into the bottom of the bath and made my-self a sort of crate covered in a survival blanket in which I sat for half an hour. That was really testing: my heart beat fast and very soon I was sweating profusely and felt dizzy. When I came out, I was a complete wreck and nearly fainting. I flopped over to lie propped upside down on my bed, as I had read that one should lie down with one's legs up to prevent varicose veins.

With all this, I started to see improvements in my rock climbing, but due to my food obsession I didn't lose a single gram in weight. Climbing with Pierre and his friends every weekend was also helping me to make enormous progress. Those lads were really very good, perhaps the best at the time. They only climbed the very hardest circuits and I was torn between pride at being accepted by them, fear of holding them back and frustration at not being up to their standard. I was far from lacking in tenacity: I sometimes had ten goes at each problem, and on circuits of 30 climbs, I might only succeed in climbing one. It was depressing but I knew I would get there one day. If others could, then so could I and I kept at it.

Some weekends, it became a personal battle between me and the rock. I became fiercely aggressive and violently angry, kicking the sandstone so hard it hurt, shouting out and crying with rage. Then, during the week, I would put twice the effort into my abdominal exercises. Some days, I had success with new climbs. How satisfying that felt. But for periods at a time, there was no improvement at all and I was in the depths of despair. I would appear to have reached a plateau for a month or two; then suddenly there would be a breakthrough. In fact I was just improving step by step and of course, the higher I raised the bar, the tougher it became.

One day, Pierre suggested we try rock climbing at Surgy. I was indeed fortunate to have such good climbers taking an interest in a kid like me. Obviously, I needed to let my parents meet him; they were thoroughly impressed with how sensible, quiet and intelligent he was. Having now obtained my passport to freedom, I could at last go away without having to lie.

Surgy is a 30 metres high limestone ridge about two hours south of Paris, in the Yonne region, which is one of the playgrounds of Parisian climbers. On a sunny weekend in spring we were sure to bump into the same crowd as at Fontainebleau, and here we all were, camping together in the field next to the cliff.

As Pierre was a much stronger climber than me, I expected to follow him, never imagining he would deign to be second on easy sections. To my great surprise however, at the foot of the cliff, he announced that we would alternate leads. Apprehensive, yet very pleased, I did not argue.

He led off on a fairly easy warm-up route. Then it was my turn and he pointed out a route. That went well too, I was in control of the situation. Over the course of the morning, we climbed six routes. It was brilliant – we were climbing as quickly as each other. In the afternoon things did not go quite so well. He suggested we try a really difficult route called the *Javanaise*. Would I be up to a climb of that level? But as Pierre was there, I put my best foot forward and went for it, thinking that if things went wrong, he would help.

Things started well and I reached first piton without any problem. The second bolt was high and it was no help being small. But after several attempts, I managed to get my foot on it and push up to get hold of the second piton; same technique on the third. At that time, this was typical rock climbing, using everything and anything to pull oneself up. After that, things became tougher: there was a tricky move by a small overhang in order to get to the next piton. After two moves on the slanting rock, my hands seemed to open of their own accord. Staring death in the face, I managed somehow to hurl myself onto the bolt and clip into it. But from there, my fingers refused to budge; frozen with fear, they could only grip the karabiner in desperation.

In absolute dread of falling, I had a burst of energy and succeeded in gathering my strength to clip the bolt with a sling attached to my harness. It was not only the fear of falling, but also of making a fool of myself in front of the many climbers watching, which had spurred me on; to let oneself fall was very bad form, and we used to say that, after three falls, a rope was fit for the bin.

What followed was just as difficult. There I was, attached to my bolt in the middle of a perfectly smooth slab and no immediate answer as to how to get hold of the next one sprang to mind. I tried all sorts of ways of getting up using the piton without any handholds to steady myself and my energy, as well as my wish to succeed, started to drain away. Down below, Pierre was calmly watching the unedifying spectacle. What was more, he was whistling one of the Bach suites, that I had been learning on my flute and rather well too. I was extremely impressed that he knew all the notes, and touched to learn that he shared my love of classical music, but it did not exactly solve my problem. Some time went past before he suggested that I take a sling, fasten it to the piton and use it as a foothold. This method is called a 'pedal' or foot loop. It did work and I was able to stand up but was still ten centimetres short of the next elusive bolt. By finding tiny holds, stretching and searching for small ledges, I did in the end manage to catch hold of it. That route was the most difficult level I could possibly have attempted, and I do not think I have ever had such a tough time before or since.

The other climbers kept looking at me. I had apparently become an object of curiosity and, when we went back to the campsite in the evening, I saw people murmuring to each other as I passed. Could I have achieved something special? I dared not ask if that route was one of the hardest. Basically I did not care. I was just relieved to have succeeded. That night I was so tired that even my prodigious appetite deserted me. I expected to sleep well but unfortunately re-lived the climb all night, and in my dreams the route was never-ending, a true nightmare.

We did the same thing for several weekends, climbing like maniacs; no fewer than ten routes a day. The other climbers could hardly believe the way we did one after the other, at top speed, alternating leads. As I managed harder and harder routes, I became increasingly motivated. From time to time, people who had watched me take climbs at a run, decided to copy me, assuming that meant it was easy. Secretly delighted to watch the idiots charging off to follow a mere girl, I savoured the way they made fools of themselves even more; as the ones who tried were not usually at that level. I thought it hilarious to watch them out of the corner of my eye as they struggled and swore for all they were worth, though I discretely did not let it show.

My Parisian friends were dreaming of going to do some big climbs and discussed taking me along. I worried that I would not be up to it and that I might hold them back, being a little sixteen year old whilst they were all between 25 and 30. When they talked, I kept in the background, listening attentively. When we were climbing, I never complained or asked them for anything. That is how in 1976 and 1977 I was lucky enough to have the opportunity to take turns leading climbs on all the most famous routes in the Verdon, even though I had never hammered in a single piton or placed a single nut. I had no idea how to use such technical gear as Clogs, Stoppers, bolts, pegs or karabiners. All that vocabulary was muddled up delightfully in my head.

Going to Verdon for the first time was a great adventure.

The routes had not been tried out very often and it was not possible to tell whether we could manage them in a day. There was an atmosphere of venturing into the unknown. We had to take with us a bag of gear in case we needed to bivouac on the face. The awkward bag snagged in the cracks and got stuck in the chimneys. After a few days of exploring, we were no longer satisfied to do just one climb a day and had the idea of doing two in a row. Or what about three? Pierre and I treated it as a huge game in which we were completely immersed. We took the routes at a run, stopwatch in hand always trying to do more. The rock had caught us up in its magic. I dared not drink or wee. His motto was not to waste time. My motto was not to be noticed. But when the need to go was just too pressing, I belayed Pierre with one hand whilst throwing myself into a great display of agility as I wriggled and struggled to get out of my harness. I would only do this on a pitch when he was lead; it was out of the question to let him see any signs of my weakness.

That holiday was utterly exhausting with not a single rest day and the worst of it was the hiking we had to do after our climbs, which were always a good ten kilometres from any car park. But I took it all in my stride, never complaining, both delighted and extremely proud of myself for covering routes at record speed. We went so fast that I forgot some of the sections or got them muddled up in my memories. When talking about it, it got difficult when other climbers were there: they mentioned a tricky bit which I could not even remember. It must be said that we were not too concerned with details: if I felt that putting in a runner was too complicated, then I just did not bother and carried on. There was one rule which Pierre insisted we obey: make sure of a good belay wherever possible and apart from that, I was free to do whatever I wanted. This rather unusual system suited me, allowing me to gain self reliance and begin to know my limits.

Caught up in the game, I wanted to go faster and faster, so I even skipped belays. When I had climbed to the end of the rope, I would shout 'belay' but actually carry on climbing at the same time as Pierre. I can't imagine he didn't notice. Another technique which fuelled this insatiability was to shout that there were ten or twenty metres of rope left when I was second, although there was in fact hardly any. That way I could climb at the same time as my leader.

We scoured the Verdon, charged through the Vercors, ripped through the Dolomites and attacked the Alps. In the latter, we set ourselves the challenge of being as committed as the earliest alpinists, whose motto was 'always start at the bottom and never say where you are going.' We never warned anyone and by preference took the least used and most inaccessible routes. We were so keen. The hardest ones were those which left from Chamonix.

We set off on foot with twenty kilo rucksacks in full knowledge that the alternative of lifts or a little train was there. It was not too bad at night, when the world was asleep and there were no trains to tempt me anyway but in the heat of the day, not using the lifts, and having to run the gauntlet of the bellowed comments from crowds of tourists about my oversized bag, took some doing. I must have had such a scowl and such a fierce expression that they did not generally keep it up for long. I took comfort from the promise of the enormous ice-cream I would eat when I returned to the valley, as a reward for our principles and our extreme frugality. It was actually very, very hard, but I still dared not complain in case Pierre thought I was a wimp. I sometimes cried from exhaustion and in fact even nowadays, I occasionally burst into tears when I am worn out. It can be quite embarrassing, as once started, I can't dam the flow of tears and people around me assume something to have gone horribly amiss.

Those testing access hikes did have their recompense: we would set up our base camp at altitude and then stay for a week scouring the area for all the 'ED' (extremely difficult) routes and even trying to do several a day. This suited me much better, as it meant less walking and more climbing. We did not eat much but absence makes the heart grow fonder and so everything we had when we got down into the valley seemed like a feast. I revelled in the well-equipped camp sites, the hot showers, the lack of rationing and, most especially, in that well-earned ice cream. In fact, if Pierre thought we had done a good hike, we treated ourselves to a second one. I have only a hazy memory of the routes and their names, but I remember doing about ten climbs per week. By the end of the season, we were up to an average of 800 metres' climbing, graded ED, per day. I especially liked leading, so most of the time Pierre let me go first out of kindness, saying that if I took a fall, being the lightest, it would be less risky to both of us.

I took great pleasure in overtaking other climbers in the middle of the route, whizzing past those fine gentlemen – such proud, tough mountaineers – like a rocket under their very noses, with just some protection every ten metres. I treated them to my most charming smile then I overtook. At the belay the gallant gentlemen left me plenty of room but if I did not like the look of them, I skipped it altogether to show off even more. I adored reaching the top first so, to make sure I would, I often cheated by skipping belays. Once there, it was bliss! I always had ready a little treat: pancakes, cakes, chocolate or best of all whipped cream mixed with sweetened chestnut purée. When these little banquets were over, we literally attacked the descent. In that, we were really kings of the mountain. We always unroped; that was another of Pierre's cardinal rules – it was better to take a dive alone than to drag one's chum down into the abyss too. That suited me just fine as, despite his long legs, I thought him a bit of a slowcoach, and when in the early days we had stayed roped to each other, he always complained that I was going too fast.

That was the way we took the measure of the Alps. I rather liked the Oisans, which, with its lack of lifts, was a land of equality, although as far as ice cream was concerned, it was sorely lacking. There were no bistros anywhere near the campsites. That was the area where I had the biggest frights though, as the rocks around the Oisans are not amongst the most solid.

The thing I found exasperating about Chamonix, was being able to see the valley. Sometimes, from our bivouac, I could see the lights twinkling down in the town, and I imagined all the people in the warmth of their chalets. How lucky they were all snug under their duvets, tucked up in a real bed... During the daytime, I sometimes wondered, 'What on earth am I doing here? Down there people are comfortably lying by a swimming pool or taking a gentle stroll through green Alpine meadows, picking wild flowers, eating raspberries, while I have to be constantly alert. And who knows how it's going to turn out this time? This is really dodgy. The tiniest slip and, woops, down we all go.'

The finest yet most challenging memories from that period are: the north face of Olan via the Couzy-Desmaison route, the north face of Ailefroide via the Devies-Gervasutti and the Dru via the American direct route. Each one of these we climbed in seven hours in July 1977. Of the three, the Dru was the hardest. We started from the bottom, right at the bottom, Chamonix, with our heavy bags, to bivouac in the pastures at the foot of the Dru face, just above the Mer de Glace. It would have been perfectly feasible to take the little Montenvers train to save 1,000 metres of altitude, but no; we were purists.

Fortunately our bivvy site was comfortable, as the dense grass made a very good mattress. Unfortunately we suffered a slight set-back early next morning when the alarm did not go off, and so were two hours late in starting on the route at around eight. Things could have turned out worse, as that morning a rockfall had sent stones hailing down onto some alpinists, who had left before us, but had to retrace their steps with one of their party injured. That was unpleasant. Affected by the accident, I no longer felt like climbing but Pierre was not to be swayed, so by midday we had reached the halfway height between the face and the jammed block.

At that point we had a short break to munch a square of

chocolate and have a drink, then we set off again climbing at top speed, one after the other: the 90 metre corner, the pendulum, another short stretch and then, a surprise, we caught up with and overtook a team who had bivouacked at the *bloc coincé*. As usual, I took the lead to overtake. They seemed disgusted. Then we caught up with a team of guides who overtly glared at me. Unfriendly, miserable blighters! Even though we knew each other by sight, they did not even say hello. I could tell that seeing us rattled them and they stopped chugging along and went past at a higher speed until... to make things worse they got tangled up in their own ropes. They had a good grumble.

To avoid further complicating their delicate manoeuvres, we headed straight up, rather than leaving by the north face. In my opinion that was the toughest and most risky section. Knowing how many climbers took the route, we had banked on finding enough pitons in place, to anchor ourselves securely and so had only brought along a few nuts. But there was nothing at all, not even a piton. After quite a few hairy moments, we got to the top at last at three in the afternoon. I was exhausted from having taken the lead all the way since the *bloc coincé* and my arms were very painful.

Going back down was trouble free and we ran the whole way, finding the instructions our friend Xavier Fargeas had given us, to be very easy to follow. Xavier was a great alpinist, who had recently succeeded in being first to climb the Dru North Couloir solo in winter. As far as I had been able to make out, this descent was supposed to be very tricky. That was why he had furnished us with a plethora of details describing the best way down to avoid problems. At last we reached the Charpoua Refuge, which was obviously in use as there were some alpinists sun-bathing on the terrace. I realised I was desperately thirsty and expected to stop and have a breather as well as a much needed drink. But before I could say anything, Pierre announced, in a voice that brooked no argument, 'No question of stopping, we're going straight down to Chamonix'.

I was complaining bitterly to myself but no one had asked for my opinion. He was older than me.

At nine in the evening we got down to the Mer de Glace. There, trying to fetch our bivouacking equipment from above the glacier, we got lost. For hours we wandered around between the crevasses, in search of the big, white rock which would show us the way to get off the glacier. But that moonlit night all the pebbles glistened white. In the end, at one in the morning, I was finished and in tears. I sat down where I was and announced that I would not budge. So we slept there, on the ice, without having eaten or drunk anything.

CLIMBING BECOMES A PROFESSION

Nothing can replace a long apprenticeship, and an accumulation of experience which become the source of intuition.

Doug Scott

Whatever could have made me climb all those major faces so madly? The mountains, the beautiful scenery? My admiration for Pierre? The physicality of rock climbing? The joy of success and effort rewarded? The well-being upon return to the valley? The constantly changing challenges, new and ever increasing in difficulty? The commitment? Certainly there was a little of all of that, and more besides, which I cannot fathom. In any case, I liked it then and I like it now.

However, now I don't like it in the same way. I am more selective about what climbs I do and the way I tackle them takes into account whatever infrastructure is available. Nowadays, I have absolutely no qualms about taking a cable car or sleeping in a mountain hut rather than outside in the cold, 100 metres away from one, nor about setting off only when the weather is favourable or only climbing on sound rock, as these are part and parcel of the conditions necessary for an enjoyable climb. I have left long behind me things like climbing piles of loose pebbles, having to be constantly wary of falling rocks, testing each hold or trembling with fear the whole way.

I am interested in the aesthetic appearance of a face and the ways to ascend it. Going hell for leather for the top no longer has any appeal. I sometimes stop just a few metres below; in any case I would already have been up there at least once before. I decide on ways up with regard to the ways back down; I need them to be uneventful. In short, what I enjoy about the mountains is pleasure, the challenge and the beauty but I do not want to sweat blood. Although, when I think back to those times when I endured so much hardship, I get a touch of nostalgia. They were exciting and they did last for four years. Four years of climbing all over, in all corners of France, Belgium, England, Switzerland, Italy...

In the midst of all that frenetic rock climbing, I still needed to settle upon a direction for my education. As far as studying went, I was a bit of a shirker; it was hard to get my head round such things when it was filled with thoughts of heading off climbing in the holidays. Nevertheless, under pressure from my climbing friends who were brilliant students from the best universities, I agreed to work on my maths and physics; what I would do in the future depended on my grades in those two subjects. I enjoyed it and most of all, doing sciences would keep doors open for a wider choice of options at a later stage.

I changed my mind on a weekly basis. I thought of being a lumberjack, a carpenter, a cabinet maker, horticulturalist, woodsman, environmental engineer, gym teacher, biology researcher, flautist, architect, model maker... In the end, I settled upon physiotherapist. I wanted to know how muscles worked and to understand the human body. Furthermore, it is a profession in which I would have the flexibility to arrange my working life as I wished and to go on holiday whenever I felt like it. Perfect! As a final deciding factor: it would involve studies which were relatively short and practical. And indeed, I had qualified by the time I was twenty.

At that point everything went to pieces. I was free, without educational constraints, able to earn money quickly and easily, able to climb when and where I wanted... Except that I no longer wanted to. What I wanted was to experience other things, move in other circles, meet new people. I was fed up with climbers and their tales of climbing, of their closed little world of gossip: 'you know Thingy? He did that route in such and such a time...'

'Yeah, but he had really good conditions for it,' or whatever. It was petty, restricted and repetitive. A world of monomaniacs. Subjects of conversation, apart from climbing, were not only rare but poor. Over the years I have observed that this was not just peculiar to the climbing world. Everyone who is fanatical about something shares their quirks with others.

So as not to break off completely, I went to get some fresh air in the forest every other month, to make sure that I had not quite lost my touch. I always managed to climb five or six difficult routes as a test of my fitness. But I hardly climbed more than ten rocks, and the rest of the time I walked or jogged. In those days I was really making my entry into another world: the world of gambling. And it was not so very different from the climbing world, all the more so as my gambling partners were climbers too. This enthusiasm started quite by accident. One rainy day, when I was sliding about miserably on the wet rocks with a few determined climbers, a voice was raised above the rain asking if anyone fancied a game of poker. It was a talented climber called Jérôme Jean-Charles – quite brilliant and a bit weird – who had just devoted two years of his life to the Rubik's cube. When he announced that he would earn money by becoming world champion, not one of us believed him. But by twisting the little cube, day and night, he did end up as world runner-up and author of two books on the subject. His passion of the moment was the statistics of poker. Weary of paddling around in the rain, we went back to Paris, for a game at his place.

That was how the poker started. Nights, whole days and yet more nights of playing. It was fascinating, extenuating, captivating, anguishing. My whole life was caught in the trap of gambling. I discovered a surprising facet of my personality: I didn't know how to bluff, even though I had told so many lies to my parents and invented so many elaborate scenarios to explain what I was up to. Sitting at a table, I found myself incapable of lying without blushing or going pale. Over many

smoke-filled nights, I turned every colour imaginable and ultimately lost on most occasions. The stakes were never high,
at the most a few Francs, but as the games went on, at the end
of the year, my losses amounted to a tidy sum.

I used to go home at seven in the morning, my head filled
with cards and with remorse, sleep for half an hour, just long
enough to have nightmares, before I went to treat my first patient at eight thirty. As the hours ticked past, I was like a zombie. At the slightest gap, even fifteen minutes, in my timetable
I stretched out on a massage table and fell asleep instantly.
When the next patient rang the bell, I woke with a start and,
jumping to my feet, I carried on as if there was nothing amiss,
praying that my body would be able to keep it up. At the end
of the day, pepped up by anticipation of the coming game, I
started to feel a lot better. In the evening on the way home, I
dreamed of making up for the previous night's losses and the
excitement made me so completely awake that, by the time I
was back at my place, there was no doubt left: I had to go and
play, I wanted to win.

The truth is that I had gone completely off the rails. I was
no longer myself. I was addicted to gambling. I was obsessed
by the anguish of losing and possessed by the desire to win.
Permanently tired, my work suffered – I was no longer able to
give my patients the same quality of attention I had previously.
I felt awful, all droopy. My face and body felt bloated and
sluggish, without sensation. Although my limbs still worked,
they did not seem to belong to me anymore. I felt fat and useless and the worse it got, the more I wanted to eat absolutely
anything at all hours. It was as if I was trying to make myself
fall apart even more, a sort of revenge or punishment for how
I had become. I was no longer even interested in clothes and
dressed without caring to look attractive. In any case, none of
my clothes fit me.

I kept imagining that my lungs were trapped in a vice, as
they would not expand properly. Walking up the stairs at the
clinic was agonising and it took me a while to catch my breath

at the top. In any free moment, I grabbed a cigarette and even made patients wait while I finished it in peace. I was smoking one or even two packets a day. It was a real disaster. I disgusted myself but was compelled to carry on gambling. When I lost, I hurried back the next night to try and make up for my losses, and when I won I hurried back even more to win again: a vicious circle. That was absolutely all I did apart from flopping in front of the television after work, before going out to gamble.

One day I weighed myself: 58 kilos. Horror of horrors! This downwards slide would have to stop. No more playing cards, no more sleepless nights, diet and exercise from now on. The new regime was a different kind of hell at first. I forced myself to go to Vincennes every day. I was in pathetic physical shape – unable to run for more than one or two minutes, with my legs so heavy and my feet refusing to lift up, risking tripping on roots. My body wibble-wobbled and I ached all over. At first I barely lasted ten minutes and went home exhausted and sweating. Due to a strict diet with no bread, pasta or sweet things, I no longer even had the consolation of stuffing my face. I was in a truly distressed state and saw this battle as the only answer. It became a permanent interior struggle.

Frequently, a little voice inside cooed, 'Come on it's too hard, stop it,' but I hung on with the strength of despair and the little self esteem I had left. I was still very tired, despite having a good nine hours sleep every night, but slowly and surely I re-emerged. Now I could keep up a half hour's run and, by the end of three weeks, I was able to go twice a day. I went for a little jog for twenty minutes at seven in the morning before work, wrapped up like an onion to work up a good sweat, then had a light breakfast of yoghurt, cracker and tea without sugar. At midday another jog, for between 30 and 40 minutes this time, but less well wrapped up. For lunch: soup, yoghurt or egg, salad. Jogging was not enough – I needed to rebuild my muscles and this was no small task. I did exercises every day without fail to get back my abdominal, back, buttock and arm muscles. Every movement was an effort and I tired quickly, still so heavy and blubbery. Hope returned the day I had lost the third kilo. At last real results! But there was still a long, hard way to go and there would be much more suffering to make myself properly fit again. The struggle eased and, importantly I was seeing some results: the exercises exhausted me less, hunger – or rather the need to feel stuffed full – no longer gnawed at my stomach. I could get back into some pairs of jeans. I went up the slippery slope with a certain pride especially since I didn't answer telephone calls from my gambling partners.

I could see the light at the end of my tunnel, but there was still something missing to be happy with life. Yes, I had a job, yes, I was a physio, but I could not see myself staying in physiotherapy forever. I started to feel that I had done all there was to do and, despite quite a variety of patients, it threatened to become merely routine. I was always doing the same treatments, using the same polite phrases and the same jokes. Patients filed past all day: grumpy ones, tired ones and sometimes dirty ones. The reality of being a professional was becoming less and less appealing. What was more, I could not see that I was really making a difference and was discouraged to see the same people with the same back problems throughout the year.

I wanted to shout at them, 'For goodness sake move if you don't want back pain.' As far as they were concerned, massages were never long enough but doing their exercises on the other hand… they hardly wanted me to prescribe any. I did my best to explain the numerous benefits of taking a bit of exercise, there was nothing doing, 'Oh, you know, once or twice with you will do, in any case, I don't have time. And I couldn't possibly let my husband see me. And I'd be worried to do the exercises wrong.'

Ultimately they were not encouraging me. I considered doing some further studying or becoming more specialised in one area of physiotherapy – sport – or even starting to study osteopathy. I was still debating what to do when, out of the blue, I got a telephone call from a small production company. They asked me to take part in a new television game called 'Enigmas from the ends of the Earth.' What was needed would be for me to climb in the Vercors, with a walkie-talkie on my head, answering the presenter's questions. This was a very well-timed offer and I jumped at it. Not having climbed for three years, it was not exactly a piece of cake but still, I had not entirely lost the knack...

That first programme was a success and the producers asked me to go on to Indonesia, Bali and then Singapore. The challenge was to run on a beach, rush into a bat cave and then prostrate myself in front of a wise man who would ask me vital questions. Even though it was silly, it made a change from my daily existence. In Singapore I had to ride a sea scooter and, caught in a storm, was submerged by giant waves. I went to ground in some mud and the sound equipment gave up the ghost. I was eliminated, but was taken on instead as a technical advisor for any episodes where they needed to use ropes. That way I was able to keep travelling and to learn what went on behind the scenes of television, with its tricks of the trade and filming methods.

I discovered new countries and met different people. I would have liked it all to last longer, but the programme was not very successful. I thought my luck had run out until the day Robert Nicod, a film maker, called me: he wanted to make a climbing film in the Verdon Gorges featuring me, as he remembered that I climbed fast. Apparently he had already called me the year before, but I had ignored it; having had several similar proposals which all came to nothing. This one was more serious and concrete, with filming due to start in June.

In those days, Robert Nicod was especially well known for his beautiful climbing photographs; no other specialist photographer of the time had such a good eye for an image. I believe he was the first photographer to have worked on a rock face and given such a feeling of the emptiness below. He was notable for having taken all the magnificent photographs of Patrick Edlinger, the famous free climber. I also knew that he had been the cameraman for two superb climbing films featuring Patrick Edlinger: *La Vie au bout des doigts* (holding life by the fingertips) and *Opéra Vertical.*

It was a tempting offer, but one which needed thought, as there would be some relatively hard climbs. He wanted to see things that had never been done before, which would need me to have a high level of fitness. This was well timed; it was now February and I would be able to stop work at the end of the month in order to go and do some training where the filming was to take place. After thoroughly weighing up the pros and the cons, I decided to embark on the adventure. As I had been paid an advance, I put my patients in the care of a colleague. It would be far from easy to meet the challenge, as my fitness could not have been lower and I had fallen badly behind on technique. That is to say that 'in my day' we all climbed on fixed routes, but since then, the game had changed. 'Free climbing' was the new fashion from the United States. The rule: not to use fixed protection to climb, nothing but the body and the rock.

During my years of debauchery, the grading systems had been extended. Levels 7a, then 7b had appeared and I would need to be able to adapt to the new rules: previously, I had scrambled for each bolt, stretching out from it to reach the next one. Now, if I wanted to be taken seriously and not risk being made fun of, I would need to adopt a 'good style.' So not only did I need to rebuild my muscles, get back my balance, re-learn how to cope with the heights, but also correct some bad habits I had got into long ago. I certainly had a plate full. On 26 March 1985, I set off in my little red Renault 5, full to the brink, to take the Verdon gorges by storm, to train and to be reborn.

My first challenge was the campsite. It was dreadfully cold. I was not properly equipped, was permanently freezing, and could not get warm. Having more pressing concerns, I was eating convenience foods and the unbalanced diet made me tired. I wondered how on earth I was to keep this up for a month. I was distraught, disenchanted and lonely as I went in search of a climber to rope up with every morning; it was a real chore. I prefer to climb with people I know and whom I trust. It bothers me to impose upon others; I worry that I will annoy them.

In those first few days, my morale could not have been lower; all the more so as I was climbing really badly – I was scared. Nothing reassured me: the ropes seemed too thin, the bolts too widely spaced and too small, the harness too insubstantial (I even used double ropes)... I was climbing like an anxious snail, taking fright at each move. What a nightmare, I was struggling at 6b. Unable to go on, petrified on my holds, it was a living nightmare and I was saying to myself, 'You must be crazy! What do you think you are doing here? Can't you see how useless you are? You're hardly going to succeed now, at your age, just give up.' I could not even think which saint I could invoke for help; I was unsure and thoroughly rattled. 'Maybe things would go better if I had a bit of comfort? Perhaps it's worth giving it a go.'

There and then I decided to book into an hotel on half board. Oh, how good it was! A hot bath every day, a comfortable bed and in the evenings, all I had to do was sit down to dinner. This turned out to be just what I needed; I relaxed and was able to concentrate on my climbing. After all, to hell with cost-cutting, I had not taken a holiday for four years and I was there to climb, not to shiver in a little tent. From then on, I got into a routine for some serious training: alarm at eight, climbing from nine to four, followed by a little jog. I had brought with me a load of weight-training gear so, back at the hotel, I did some energetic push-ups with weights to round off the day. At six in the evening I soaked in a nice, hot bath with a book; dinner was at seven-thirty; at eight I collapsed into a deep sleep.

Little by little I made progress. After ten days, I managed to do some 6c free climbing, then five days later a 7a. I began to enjoy life once more and to have fun. I loved climbing again, especially this free climbing, which was like a new game. Some old friends from Fontainebleau took turns to come and join me. For them it was an opportunity for a few days' break and, for me, to be able at last to climb in harmony, to talk about certain climbing sections and share my feelings with friends.

My only worry was whether or not I would be up to climbing the Bombé de Pichenibule, around 7b/c, which Robert insisted on filming. The first time, I could not find the holds and did not make a single move. What was more, it was an exceptionally impressive place with fabulous views. How could I expect to get up that section seeming relaxed if I was like a sausage dangling from a rope and couldn't even decode the puzzle? But I carried on training with determination for a month and a half without giving up, and am rather proud of myself for it. Sometimes it got really lonely in the evenings in my little hotel room; there were not many people around the Gorges du Verdon and I was often the only guest at the hotel. It was a bit spooky sitting alone in the dining room. I was constantly anxious, it was not in the bag yet; I had made progress but maybe I had made a bet too hard to win?

For a film, you have to be able to climb fast and smoothly, in order to get good images. Robert had given me the details of the screenplay with the routes he intended to film – the easiest section was a 6b/c level. Each day, I worked on one of the sections which would be filmed. On very cold or windy days it was hard work. Nevertheless I carried on, practising time and again, convinced that it would eventually sink in. It was the Bombé de Pichenibule which was the most problematic; I kept falling off. I became obsessed by it and went over and over the moves in my head every night. It was always the same section which gave me nightmares: outside of left foot on a very tiny edge, right foot toe in an open crack; right hand on a tiny crimp, then throw the left hand up. Then, right hand next to me, bring feet together below it, big push; middle finger of right hand and jam left hand in the crack. Phew! Clip on and breathe. Then, one day, miracle of miracles, I did it! What a relief! I was thrilled to have proved up to the challenge.

With nothing more to do I returned to Paris the same evening. Fed up with the Verdon, with the hotel, with the tough routine and with being tense. I drove back to Paris singing all the way. It had been a long time since I had felt so happy, fulfilled and in good shape.

In Paris, I went everywhere looking for a climbing outfit. Robert wanted me to wear a swimming costume with an open back. These were only just beginning to come into the shops and the choice was limited. The rope which Michel Béal had supplied for me was dayglo pink: how was I to find an outfit which went with such a bright colour? I was looking for a swimming costume in a shade of candy pink. I wonder if the hardest part of all my preparation for that film wasn't trawling all over Paris trying to find the right costume. There is nothing more gruelling than trying on a dozen outfits a day, looking at oneself in the mirror just as often, checking the tiniest detail. Something was always wrong: straps that were too thin; or when I lifted my arms up – peepo – my breasts popped over the top of the costume; or the front was not wide enough and after a few minutes of moving – peepo! – breasts out at the sides; or although the costume fitted perfectly, it had horizontal stripes, which are not flattering, and so on... The sales assistants were vile; exasperated by the picky, wriggling customer. At long last I found one I liked. Everything was right: the top, the straps, the material, the colour. Everything except the fact that it was a thong, with just a string between my buttocks: a bit too risqué for my first film! I could not face any more shops, the top was perfect and I would just have to wear shorts to hide the cheeky little string...

Filming time was approaching, so the whole cast and crew met up in Paris before going down to the Gorges du Verdon. There were not many of us – just five – and that suited me. There was Philippe the sound engineer, Patrick the photographer, Robert the film-maker and cameraman, Joël the assistant and me. Only Monique Dalmasso, my climbing partner,whom I only knew from photographs, had yet to arrive. I was a bit sorry not to have met her before and hoped she did not turn out to be awful and that she did not take herself too seriously. I sometimes get bad tempered and have difficulty holding my tongue. From the first time we met, in the Verdon, all my apprehension evaporated and we soon became firm friends.

On the first days of filming, we all got to know one another. Philippe, who was in charge of sound recording, had never done this before; he was a nurse. Patrick had never before been up a rock face and had never taken photographs of climbing; Monique had only been climbing for six months and Robert, the film cameraman had only ever filmed as assistant cameraman on two sets which each lasted three days. This all came as a bit of a surprise, if not a worry. On the first day they were reading the instruction manuals for the camera and recording equipment. There were differences of opinion on how to thread the film into the camera... In any case, we could not have done anything else as the weather was too bad. So we remained confined to barracks, in bedrooms, inspecting and prodding all the peculiar equipment: cameras, lenses, mikes, sunshade, darkroom bag... When each of us had familiarised himself with his tools, we moved on to practical sessions.

Robert Nicod was used to working on the rock face and was amazingly quick at getting set up. He was the inventor of the 'goat'. At first, when he mentioned using a goat in the film, I had some idea that he would be arranging little nanny goats on ledges... In fact the 'goat' he was talking about was an ingenious device comprising two long booms which allowed the camera and its operator to be moved away from the face in order to pan out and increase the impact of the image. It was vertiginous and I admit that I would not have wanted to change places with him, perched like that, right over the drop. He accepted it with equanimity and was in complete control.

Philippe, the sound recordist was a climber himself and knew how to get into position without assistance. There was a slight problem though – he did not always place himself correctly in relation to the camera and the microphone sometimes appeared in shot. But as for the photographer, that was quite another kettle of fish. First, it took at least half a day just to get him into his harness. He never felt comfortable in it – his lordship was worried that his sensitive bits would be crushed, and ingenious and elaborate adjustments were needed to put it on. Sometimes we heard Patrick shrieking with pain from the rock face. Next we needed to teach him to abseil down by belaying himself, to clip on to the belay, and to go back up with ascenders. Poor thing, I don't think he will ever forget it, especially as the Gorges du Verdon are hardly ideal for learning this kind of thing; it is the most impressive place I know.

The vertical cliffs are smooth and the mountain stream rumbles from way down below. Patrick was trying very hard to overcome his fear and did not always listen properly to what we were telling him. He would rush off without paying proper attention to safety, or do the right things, but in the wrong order. Often, right in view of the camera, he would shout for help: 'Robert, Robert, what do I do now?' Once, during a take, I found myself next to him. It was horrifying; he was balanced on a tiny step with no rope to hold him, his cameras dangling from his neck (there were four of them, which prevented him from seeing his feet).

It is a miracle that we never saw our Patrick going past in free-fall. I do think that on that day he actually understood what danger he was in and, subsequently, he called out to us from all over the place for someone to go and attach him, or unclip him or check the knots in his ropes, etc. At the end of the day, he was always the first to scarper, and only got colour back in his cheeks and his voice back down to its normal pitch once we were back at the hotel having our evening meal. On the face, we tired of his incessant questions, in addition to the volleys of click-clunk noises from his cameras, which made synchronised sound recording tricky. Robert had planned to take fifteen days to film, but as it was raining most of the time, we decided to stop and come back in June, praying for the weather to show more clemency.

A month later there we all were again, nose to the grindstone. Nearly all that is – the photographer could not face it again and we had changed sound-recordist as the nurse was sitting his exams. Marvellous, it was sunny; but oh, so cold. We could not film in the sun, to avoid having the shadow of the hoist on the face, but the shade did not come round until late afternoon. At an altitude of 1,000 metres, in the late afternoon, wearing a swimming costume it was chilly; exceedingly so. Poor Monique stood at the end of the pitches with chattering teeth as she belayed me. There was only one camera and we frequently had to re-do the takes several times. At first she coped with the cold in silence, but over time her stoicism waned. She was worn out and was wasting away before our very eyes. Our job to be 'climbing actresses' became harder and harder and needed enormous reserves of concentration.

When filming was over, I decided to allow myself another few days off before returning to work and to my patients. I went to Chamonix to join my new boyfriend Lothar, whom I had recently got to know in the Gorges du Verdon. Those few days spent with him messed up all my plans. I was expecting to go back to Paris, spend the summer doing physio cover work and then, once the film came out, try and get some stunt jobs on film sets and maybe even try a circus school. Lothar did not seem particularly impressed and advised me to continue climbing and to enter for the very first rock climbing competition which was to take place in Italy a week later. What a ridiculous idea! Whatever was he thinking? A competition? I had always been dead against them.

But he craftily won me over reasoning that only fools never change their minds and that I would never really know what they were like unless I tried one to see. Perhaps he was right? He added 'Anyway, you'll win and it will be a good way to get known and promote the film too.' I was not so sure about that. What did he know about it? I thought it highly unlikely that I would win, having only taken up climbing again three months before and I assumed that the other girls would have improved. But still, by suggesting it Lothar had put me in a quandary and I did not know what to think. To cap it all, I had been signatory to a petition against competitions two years previously, and it had been published. How ironic!

Climbing had evolved as a rare competition-free sport and by signing the article, we had tried to keep it that way for as long as possible. The nineteen signatories were all excellent climbers, among the best of their time. I did suspect that some of them preferred to keep their reputation via the misty route of rumour ('Did you hear that so and so managed to...?') than via an indisputable grading. If the fraternity engenders reputations, competition sanctions them: there are winners and also losers. What this meant, was that way the sport operated would be quite different. Climbers would cease to be eccentric outsiders and the race for sponsorship would become vicious. No longer would one be known for having opened up exceptionally hard routes, one would have to win on a given day. The thing about competitions is that only one person wins.

So our original attitude was reactionary: we did not want competitions in order to preserve our own games and our privileges. The little paragraphs on how over-used sites would be at competition time were, in my opinion false pretexts. On reflection, I understood that my real argument was based on something much more personal: I was actually afraid to confront others. In the end, I decided that if I did not go to the competition I would just be chickening out.

'Come on old girl, it won't do you any harm to have your feathers ruffled a bit. The time of competitions has arrived. If you want to have a place in climbing, you'll need to jump on the bandwagon.' I posted my entry form the next day. That action was a big step to take, because it meant I was committed. Five days before the ordeal, I still did not believe it, yet there we were in the minibus on our way to Bardonecchia. It was madness. What was I thinking?

In Italy, the event seemed to be very important – I could not believe my eyes. There were posters and banners announcing the competition which was to take place in the wonderful valley of the Paroi des Militaires, between Italy and France. What a set up! Tapes to guide people, huge marquees erected in a field with numbered tents around them in serried rows, enormous trucks covered in adverts, rubbish skips, and even shower and toilet blocks by the mountain stream. The rock face was striped in all directions by big strips of red, yellow and green tape. I was quite overcome by everything. I was staring, absolutely appalled, when a face suddenly popped up at the car window, grinning from ear to ear.

'Hi Catherine. So, you dropped by for a visit? We haven't seen you for ages.' Huh, I had been spotted – that put me in a bad mood. Shame on me for taking part in this big circus. Very few people knew I was back in climbing. I had avoided getting in touch, as I had not been in the mood for talking about how I was getting on and what I was up to. It was really unfortunate to have bumped into him. I gave a grunt and a glimmer of a smile and begged Lothar to take me away from this place, as I could not bear it. As we went along, all I could see was faces I recognised.

It was unbelievable, even though I had been away for so many years, all the same people were there. I had no wish to renew my acquaintances under these circumstances. I was embarrassed by the way I was making my official return to the climbing world. I sent Lothar off to take a look at the notice boards and he reported back that I was not up for another four days. I did not fancy being left to stew in an atmosphere like this, so we decided to take off and do a bit of climbing, near Briançon. In fact I had not done any climbing for over three weeks and suspected that I had put on a bit of weight again.

On the cliff at Pouit, I got back into my old ways of climbing when I was with Pierre. We climbed all the routes systematically, in good style, that is to say free climbing. It took us two days. In the evenings I jogged for between twenty minutes and half an hour. My theory was, that if I climbed as much as I possibly could, until I was utterly exhausted, for two days and then had two days' rest, I would be on top form. As for food – two days of dieting on the climbing days and then top up for maximum energy. The day before the competition, we treated ourselves to a restaurant meal in Italy. I adore pasta and literally stuffed myself before finishing with a huge ice cream. It felt so good to be able to eat what I wanted with a clear conscience...

We had previously spotted a quiet place for our camper van, as going to park alongside the tents was out of the question. I was imagining myself peacefully settled in a little grassy clearing next to the mountain stream. Imagine our horror when, barely on the track to the field, our headlights shone on tents and huge motor homes packed together with people on the ground in sleeping bags scattered all over. I was furious for getting myself into this. I had but one wish: to escape. After driving around at night for over an hour, we found a spot which would do; maybe less private than I wanted, but at least it was near the stream, in other words near water as I have an obsession with having to wash my hair before I go climbing. The people I am with laugh at me, but if I don't, I feel as if I can't move properly, even though sticking one's head in a mountain stream at seven in the morning is far from enjoyable.

By eight I was standing in front of the reception tent. When I gave my name, all eyes which had hitherto been concentrating on paperwork, swivelled to gawp. I did not know where to put myself; they looked me up and down from head to toe and hurried to shake my hand, thanking me profusely for being there. Embarrassed, I managed to sketch a smile and mumble a few words. They registered me and then gave me my starting times and competitor number. Surprise, I was not on until the following day. There were so few girls, that the qualifying rounds had been cancelled. I was disappointed, as I was all psyched up for that day. Never mind, I would go and watch the boys competing. It was still early and there were not many people around. We decided to go and walk around the foot of the cliff. We had scarcely slipped past the tape that spectators were supposed to keep behind, than two members of staff on security duty pounced on us. It was forbidden to walk here because there was an organised competition.

'Oh really? Thanks for telling us, sorry, we didn't realise.' We asked questions about how it was organised. They had been keeping a watch on the cliff day and night for two weeks, to make sure no one took the climbs which had been set up for the competition. They told us what they were worried about; namely that the cliff was crumbling a bit in places and had needed to be tidied up to avoid rock falls. Five new routes had been opened specially for the event, each one presenting a certain level of complexity. Girls and boys would use two shared routes: one 6c and one 7a. The boys' final route was classed 7b and the girls' 7a. Judging would include speed, style and level of difficulty.

We thanked the kind gentlemen warmly and retreated to blend in with the crowds of spectators which were starting to arrive. I tried not to be recognised; the carnival atmosphere was making me rather ill at ease. Fortunately, I had not dressed up as a trendy climber, in the latest dayglo colours, so I went quite unnoticed. Armed with binoculars and huddled against a pile of rocks, I settled down behind the crowd. For this first international contest, all the participants were allowed to observe the cliff and the other competitors in action in any way they wanted. It turned out to be a hard and anxious day for me. As all the candidates took their turns, I became progressively paler and paler, with a knot in my stomach. With each new climber, my pulse raced suddenly, as much for them as for myself, as I knew what they were going through.

My desire to compete ebbed away as I saw how so many people were watching, applauding and judging. How dreadful! Would I even remember how to climb with all that going on? Some of them seemed to be panicking and climbed frantically and awkwardly. Others were the opposite, seeming very calm and sure of themselves. Up to now, nearly all the boys had managed the 6c. I was slightly cheered up by seeing among them a few who were not as good as me. However, the 7a section was another kettle of fish: several strong climbers took a long time to work it out and many of them fell right at the top. I tried to make out the holds with my binoculars, but it was impossible; it was too far away. In any case, as I was not as tall, I would certainly not be able to manage the same moves. I was getting more and more stressed out. And to think that tomorrow it would be my turn to clown around in front of the staring crowd. Now it was time for the last contestant. Quick! I needed to duck away before the others, to avoid being caught up in the crowds and the need to talk to all the people I knew.

We were at last away from all that, alone in the mountains. In a panic at what was waiting for me the next day, I spent several hours deep in thought, unable to move or take any decisions. It was basically fear of not being up to it and of losing which was hitting me so hard. I felt ridiculous for being so afraid, but I could not help it. It was out of the question to pull out now; I had taken the decision to take part and not to go would be cowardly. With great kindness and without saying a word, Lothar got busy with preparing dinner. I made an effort to calm down and got my gear ready to face the challenge. In fact it was just my harness and climbing boots, but the latter were a real problem. The soles were all worn away and what little remained was coming unstuck. I could have climbed in new boots but they would have needed to be worn in.

Against all expectations, I had a good night's rest. In the morning, scared stiff, I presented myself for the first challenge – speed. Like a zombie, as soon as the number had been pinned on to my back, I roped up and then, at the signal, charged rather than climbed – without thinking, automatically. I was so surprised to reach the top so soon that I forgot to stop the stopwatch. Everyone was screaming. Judging by their reaction, it was a good time. The next challenge – difficulty.

A 6b came first. It did not look too tough. The girls coming down were beaming; it had been OK for them. This was the event for which spectators had turned up in their hundreds. It was impressive to see them at the foot of the routes. They followed each climber, shouting encouragement when they showed signs of flagging, applauding every time they clipped on to a piton. When the climber reached the top, the crowd went wild.

In two minutes it would be my turn. I was getting increasingly twitchy; I would need to concentrate to coordinate my movements. Oh hell! I could not remember how to put on my harness. I was turning it every which way. Bloody tangled-up harness – how could it do that to me, in front of all those people? At last I managed to get my legs into the leg loops. Bad luck – it was inside out. I struggled to get out of the thing quickly, before everyone realised. In my head, I was swearing like a trooper. Whilst muttering and telling the whole world what I thought of it, I succeeded in getting my legs so tangled up they could not move and ended up falling flat on my face on the scree. Well done! It would have been hard to find a better way of being noticed. Trying not to look disconcerted, I gave a faint smile to the people around me and took some deep, calming breaths. Sensibly now, from a sitting position, I laid the wretched thing out on the ground, put both feet into the correct holes and succeeded in strapping the whole lot on.

When my name was called, I got up carefully. All that remained was to rope up. My hands were shaking so much that I could not tie a single knot properly and in the end, the person in charge of belaying the candidates tied them for me in fits of laughter. I could not have felt less like laughing. I wished I could be swallowed up into the earth. At the start signal I was off like an arrow. It was really very easy and my partner was practically telling me off, shouting, 'Hey! It's not a race.'

The second climb a 6c. Despite the warnings, I was still climbing too fast and went the wrong way. I had to come back down a metre, but got to the top with ease. Finally just the 7a was left. Up to now, none of the girls had succeeded. The two previous routes had calmed me down and given me back some confidence. Now for my turn. I determined to tie my own boot-laces and give the knot my best shot and nothing went wrong – an excellent start. I climbed like a machine, smoothly and without once hesitating. Each time I belayed, the crowd went crazy. I passed the overhang at which many others had fallen. Super, it was over. I was careful not to lose concentration on the two metres remaining, and then I was at the chain at the top of the route. People were screaming, applauding and when I got down all the photographers raced up to me. I barely had room to take off my boots.

The guy who had belayed me, told me that I had been fastest out of all the competitors – boys and girls combined. Although I was pleased, I could think of only one thing and that was leaving. Just after me, an Italian managed the route, so we were the only two girls to have done the whole thing. I had two more ordeals to get through: the prize-giving and the questions from journalists who jumped on me asking about the manifesto against competitions. My frank reply pulled the rug from under their feet. I quoted Lothar's, 'Only fools never change their minds.' I said I had come to see for myself what climbing competitions were like.

As far as this first one was concerned, I had done what I had set out to do and we decided to spend the summer in the mountains; at first in Chamonix and then in the Dolomites. I was delighted to be going back to my first love. The 13 July saw us happily on the train to Montenvers, with only a light back-pack, ready to take on the crowd at the refuge and then the faces of the Envers-des-Aiguilles. On the morning of 14 July, the weather was beautiful, not a cloud in the sky. At 8am, we left the refuge in no hurry to try the 'Pyramid', a climb which started only five minutes away. Feeling super fit, I was burst-ing with anticipation of the climb. So, when I caught a glimpse of the granite face warming in the sun, I was so excited that I rushed out onto the snow to get to the foot of the climb as quickly as possible. Five metres away from the rock, as I stopped to admire the face and start to make out the route, Lothar came up to me and said, 'Come on, let's go down a bit to change our boots.' I thought to myself, 'Why bother to go down and change on the snow, when there's a nice, sunny rock terrace just at the bottom of the face?'

Without stopping to think, I headed off to the platform. The second I stepped over the gap between the glacier and the rock, the snow gave way suddenly underneath me and everything happened very fast after that. I realised that I had made a really serious blunder: I had actually forgotten that I was on a glacier. Everybody knows that in-between the glacier and the rock there is a crevasse. This is in fact a hole which, depending on the season, can either be filled up or can be up to 200 metres deep in places. At that instant, I thought, 'I hope it's not too deep.' I was already anticipating a sheepish climb back out, hoping that Lothar would not have noticed...

Unfortunately, the hole turned out to be an abyss and I passed out. I am not sure at what point that happened: either as I actually fell or maybe as I realised that it was bottomless. Poor Lothar was suddenly all alone. He had heard nothing more than a 'wump'; I had stopped myself from crying out so he would not notice what I had done. He understood immediately. He called: no reply. He looked down: only darkness. It was important to act very quickly, as an injured person in a crevasse can become rapidly and dangerously chilled. To top it all, the ropes were in my rucksack, but fortunately another group of climbers were nearby. They had already climbed one pitch but descended at top speed to help Lothar. That must have been the most agonising time for him.

He went down, down, and further down into that dark hole, finding out just how deep it actually was. He must have thought I was dead. Only as he reached the bottom, his eyes adjusting to the low light levels, did he make out a red splodge on the snow: my trousers. He only saw my legs at first, as the rest of me was tipped over an edge where the hole went yet deeper. With great difficulty, he tried to move me. Pulling my legs he caused so much pain that I started to regain consciousness. If he had not come down, I think I would have fallen asleep forever, numbed by the cold. It was not unpleasant; I was dreaming and would not have felt anything. Perhaps death is not so bad after all...

Apparently I kept asking the same questions, but I can only remember the last few answers as Lothar repeated the same things, over and over. It was the words 'Pyramide', 'climbing', 'Envers des Aiguilles' which brought me round. Now that I was awake, I started to think about getting back up the crevasse. At first glance, it did not look difficult; despite the cold and the pain, it looked possible... But I had not yet thought to take stock of my body. It seemed that Lothar was keener than I to know what shape I was in. He told me that the rescue services had been called and were on their way. I was relieved by the idea a helicopter coming to fetch me. Used as I was to years of mountaineering without ever dreaming of calling for a helicopter, I had forgotten that such a possibility even existed.

I then checked my body, first the hands: ripped off nails and a big gash on the little finger of my right hand but in reasonable working order. Arms, elbows, shoulders all fine. I could move my legs, so no paralysis and my spine was perhaps undamaged. My right thigh hurt a great deal and I tried to lift it – it moved, so no breakage. Phew! Otherwise I would not have been able to stand for three to four months. However, my hip seemed to be damaged. It hurt terribly each time I put weight on my right leg to sit up a little. Things could have been worse, I had got away with relatively little damage. As for the hip, if it was not dislocated, it would only take three to four weeks. What a stupid waste of time. How angry I was with myself. To have messed myself up like this. My summer was done for and what was more, so was Lothar's. But blaming myself was not going to make any difference.

It was true that, if I had listened to him, this would never have happened. The pain and the cold were bringing me to my senses. Now that I had notice the injury and irreversibility of the situation, the temperature started to worry me seriously. Lothar had put two pullovers on me but I was still shivering and the trembling set off the pain. I wanted the helicopter to come and to come quickly, to take me to hospital. The rescue services arrived at last. A man with a moustache came down on the end of a rope and, after the briefest of greetings, took stock of my breakages. He was worried about my spine. I grumbled a little: 'No, no, it's OK.' In any case, he paid no attention to me and called for a basket stretcher. I was praying for my spine to be undamaged. If not, the situation would be quite different and I could look forward to a life of pain. He also asked for a neck brace. There, I thought he really was going too far. I had been moving my head in all directions without any pain for over an hour. But he brushed away my protests and I found myself quickly and efficiently packaged up.

They sent a cable down and I was at last hoisted back up into the daylight with my moustachioed saviour. Lothar was still down below and had a quite a wait, shivering with cold, before being brought up. What a pleasure it was, to be back in the light and the warm sunshine. The first thing I saw as I came out was the granite and its pure lines. I still wanted to climb but felt really weak. I was surrounded by a lot of people, some of whom I recognised from the refuge the day before. They had peculiar expressions; they must have thought I was dead, as the cable's winch had registered 35 metres' depth – the equivalent of a twelve storey building... From their air of contrition, I sensed that they did not put a particularly high value on my life.

Before lifting me into the helicopter, I was offered a morphine injection, but I refused; wanting to stay conscious. In the helicopter, I thought of Lothar, all alone with two bags to carry back down to the valley, and worried sick about me. I didn't know him very well, and it upset me to cause him so much bother. This had happened because I was in such a hurry and due to my own negligence. If only I had listened. Now I would need to heal and recuperate quickly. How cold I was. Were we nearly there yet? The helicopter set down and two men in white coats took charge of the stretcher and heaved it into a van. At the hospital at last, now came the most painful part of the whole accident. They put me on a very uncomfortable trolley and then undressed me to take me to be X-rayed. Every movement was agonising. I was cold already but this was even worse. I lay naked on the table, waiting in anguish for the X-ray results: I had explained that I was a physiotherapist.

After a few minutes, the verdict came: double fracture of the hip. I asked whether my spine had been damaged and was told that I had an old fracture on the first lumbar vertebra. Strange. How could I have had a spine injury without noticing? Well, why not, after all, I had had so many falls at Fontainebleau, it was possible. Nothing had shown up on my painful left ankle either. I had got away without much damage though I needed my head and little finger sewing up: sixteen stitches in my head and three for the finger. Now off to bed in the recovery suite. My temperature had fallen very low to 35°C. The nurses took wonderful care of me, piling on blankets and surrounding me with hot water bottles.

What I enjoyed less, was a drip, as I cannot stand injections. Two or three hours later, I was already much better and had a normal temperature when Lothar arrived looking as if he had been through the wringer. His face was worn with worry and tiredness, he had not had time to change and his T-shirt was covered with blood. To reassure him, I spoke of my fractures, saying that in theory, I would be up and functioning normally in a month. He did not seem to believe me and smiled kindly replying, 'Well, we'll see.' I was in a dilemma as to whether my parents should be told straight away, or later when I was a bit more presentable. Worrying that they might find out from the newspapers, I decided to break the news myself, by phone.

I talked about the weather, a bit embarrassed to say what had happened, but told them in the end that I had had a little accident in the mountains and was calling from the hospital, but that everything was fine, it was not serious, etc. Mum wanted to come and I tried to tell her that there was no need, that I was well looked after and had a friend with me (they had not yet met Lothar). I only succeeded in putting off their visit for one night.

They turned up the next day, pale and dishevelled. They were shocked to see my black eye and grazed face, but thought I was generally not doing too badly. I was struggling like a demon to eat peas whilst lying down in bed. They were rolling all over the place, everywhere but into my mouth. I was furious because I was famished. Seeing me complaining so loudly was a great comfort to them, but that did not prevent my mother from falling ill as soon as she returned to Paris. Those were the repercussions.

I stayed in hospital for two weeks, at the end of which I was also diagnosed with a broken rib. The two weeks went well. I was like royalty with all of Chamonix filing through my bedroom to pay court to me. I was thoroughly spoiled, so much so that I was afraid of gaining weight. Everyone brought gifts of cakes and sweets and I knew I would need to get climbing again soon. Only Lothar brought cheese and yoghurts (special Swiss ones if you please) to get my bone calcium levels up quickly. I started walking on crutches two days before I came out. To tell the truth, I was no longer really listening to the doctors, who were all coming out with different opinions, and I preferred to trust my own experience as a physiotherapist to start my recuperation.

It was only after I left the hospital, that I understood the full extent of the damage. I had no strength in my legs and was stiff as a poker, unable to put on socks or trousers by myself. My legs were stick thin. On the evening I came out, we went out for a meal and the nightmare began. It was impossible to stay in a sitting position for more than two or three minutes; a dull pain in my back meant that I needed to push all my weight on the table with my elbows to alleviate it. By the end of the meal, I could hardly lift an elbow to be able to eat. Lothar kept asking, 'Are you OK?' He was so pleased that I was out of hospital, but also unhappy to see me in such a pathetic state. I replied, 'It'll get better.'

A month later, I was back on the rock face. In any case, it was best way of exercising to get back in shape. For a broken hip, one should allow three weeks' healing time, so this was about the right time to start returning to my normal activity level.

To be perfectly honest, I was not feeling brilliant and my back was still horribly painful. Much as I tried, the pain was impossible to ignore. One day, I plucked up the courage to have my back X-rayed. As I suspected, there was a spinal fracture, but it was a recent one. The image even showed a small fragment of bone just in front of a vertebra. The Chamonix hospital had really not done its job properly. Now it was too late to attempt any surgery, as I had already been upright and moving for over a month. I decided to start physiotherapy treatment immediately, that is to say muscular strengthening. At that time, there were articles about me springing up all over the media, which bothered me.

After the Bardonecchia competition and the release of *E pericoloso sporgersi* (It's dangererous to lean out of a moving train), the film made in the Gorges du Verdon, journalists were still saying I was the best female climber in the world; ignoring the fact that I had had this accident. How preposterous! I could barely move any more. Worse still: climbing world people were witnessing how useless I was! All I could do was avoid well-used cliffs and practise somewhere tucked away, in an attempt to regain a bit of strength, confidence and flexibility. The goal I set for myself for that year was to win another competition. I needed to catch up with the image that the press were creating of me. I was equally bothered by all the photos of me that were being published. Were these images trying to show off my body, or what I was capable of and why so many of them?

During that time, manufacturers of equipment and clothes were giving me samples of their wares: climbing boots, harness... It was amazing. I was delighted yet somewhat surprised to be receiving so many presents. 'Would you like trousers, would you like a pullover?' I replied, 'No, no I couldn't possibly accept.' They insisted and I did not know how to refuse, so accepted awkwardly, thanking them profusely. One day Lothar, who had an excellent head for business and had himself created a highly successful clothes label 'Lothars Paris' in the 1960s, accompanied me on a visit to one of the manufacturers. When they tried to give me a pair of climbing boots, Lothar asked, 'How much will you pay her to wear them?' How awful – I did not know where to look – I wished I wasn't with him and wanted to sink into the floor. Me, who hardly knew how to accept things.

The person was obviously not expecting that. He was a bit surprised, but recovered very quickly, 'Well yes, we can give that some thought.' I could not believe what I was seeing and hearing. Pay me to climb in their boots? It didn't seem to be the done thing, but he was prepared to think about it. I will never forget that conversation in which they talked terms for over an hour. Each one tested the waters in turn, evaluating the other until, after a while Lothar said, 'I reckon it's worth such and such a price.' I was really too astonished to say anything that day. All I could do was stare at Lothar. No, he was not joking and the man was only protesting feebly. In my opinion this conversation was unreasonably greedy. I hadn't yet understood that with each mention in the press, I was helping to publicise the company and as my name was all over the media, I represented a good product.

Despite everything it took me some getting used to. Lothar would not let me open my mouth when he was negotiating a contract. Once, when he came up with a price, I could not help bursting out laughing. Another time I thought he had overdone

it and exclaimed, 'But Lothar, that's too much!' I must admit
that our business partners were delighted and he, poor thing,
had to work hard to retrieve his position. So, to each their role.
From potential sponsors, I made sure to choose products I
liked and manufacturers I was comfortable to work with. If I
identified one, I went straight to them and suggested that we
work together. In that way, I was quite happy to represent
them and also to give feedback on their products. Lothar only
took take care of the financial side – but it was a vicious circle.
Sponsorship is all fine and good but you also have to fulfil
your side of the bargain. I had become a professional climber.
Sponsors targeted me because of my many appearances in the
media, but you only get mentioned if you stay at the top of
your game. I think that at the time all that took off, I did not
actually deserve it. After my fall in the crevasse, I was barely
rock climbing and my level was mediocre to say the least. I
did not even know whether I would be able to climb, or do
competitive climbing as before. After all, the people and journalists who reckoned I was the best, did so merely on the
strength of one film and one competition.

In fact, I was benefiting from Patrick Edlinger's fame. It
was thanks to him that the media and general public had become interested in rock climbing. I was included with him, but
as a female version. What a boon for the newspapers. A girl
who climbs bare-handed, how about that, and what's more,
she's not too bad looking either – alas yes – that makes a difference.

To come to terms with all this media hype, I threw myself
into intensive training in order to regain a good level. Once
more I did long sessions of weight training, rock climbing,
running and stretching. It meant a great deal of work and not
a lot of fun or time off, no time for feelings, reading or music
anymore: I was becoming a machine. At first, I could not even
do climbs which just used to be warm ups before the accident.
I was literally petrified, even though I had done them solo
before, and could not climb as much as one or two metres

properly – I was trembling like a leaf and was afraid of falling. It would certainly not have been a good idea if I fell, as I was still fragile. Occasionally, I even needed to pull on a sling in order to reach the next one. I was rigid with fear and tearful with despair. One day, I met a friend who had been in the same sort of accident three years previously and had never since been able to climb as before. I was shattered but refused to accept it and decided to fight. So, little by little, it started to come back. It was not until March the following year that I started to climb routes again without apprehension. For bouldering it was longer; it took me two years and, even now I am sometimes afraid on certain rocks. But, generally speaking, I was not doing too badly. It was hard and I believe it was my physiotherapy expertise that helped me to get there.

The next summer, I went back to the second international competition at Bardonecchia. I was stressed, of course, but had more determination than before as I now had things to prove, both to myself and to others. They were waiting for me. Although now on quite good form, I knew that it was not a foregone conclusion as, this time, the strongest climbers from all over the world would be competing, most notably the American, Lynn Hill. I had heard that she was the first woman ever to have climbed a 7c and that she was a formidable adversary. I was impressed but not too worried. From careful reading of the rules, I knew that the highest graded climb was only a 7a+ and that we would be allowed three tries at it. Furthermore, if several of us succeeded in reaching the top, then timing would be taken into account. In theory, 7a+ would not pose a problem for me. I could therefore aim for speed, which was my strong point anyway.

As it turned out, that was how I won. I was very sorry as far as Lynn was concerned; she had done the same climbs as me and on the last one, I had fallen twice, through trying to go too fast, before succeeding. I had nevertheless taken much less time than her. The very peculiar ruling did not at all reflect the way in which we free-climbed. I was not proud of having won like that but that was the way it was – I had stuck to the rules of a competition. If Lynn was unaware of that rule, she must have felt very hard done by. I would have liked to have talked to her, but at the time my English was worse than inadequate and she could not yet speak a word of French.

Having returned from the competition, I succeeded on a climb graded 8a, which was the hardest that any girl had ever done so far. But now that I was a professional climber, it was not always easy to go climbing whenever I wanted. I had to juggle between: interviews with journalists from the press; from television and radio; screening events for the film; society cocktail parties; show-biz weekends which I needed to attend to promote my sponsors and my brand image. That was not counting the many offers that I had to consider carefully before accepting, all of which prevented me from concentrating on my training. It all caused me so much stress that I was unable to progress any longer. As soon as I went away to a climb, not only did I feel ill-at-ease but what was more, a gaggle of curious onlookers were in my wake to see Destivelle in action. (They are still there but it no longer gets to me.)

How could I forget to mention all the photo shoots? It was all very serious and restrictive, demanding great attention to detail to ensure that I was wearing the right clothes so that my sponsors got promoted and the product seen properly, with the logo showing and everything matching as much as possible. That is to say that the logos had to be sewn on all visible angles, but to try not to look like a woman smothered in them. Then a nice place had to be found, with nice structures in the background and, most importantly, good light – all that was before taking the demands of some newspapers into account. Once, in the middle of winter, they wanted summer photos: on no account would old images be accepted, they had to be brand new, partly on account of the sponsors. So I had to smear myself with smelly self-tan cream. On top of everything, the light had to be summery. We thought we had got it all right on the first session, until someone noticed that the trees in the distance had no leaves; which meant starting all over again.

In spite of it all, deep down I did not feel I deserved all that was happening to me. The moment I went off climbing somewhere, articles and photos were spread all over the magazines. Even if I accepted this kind of exhibitionism – as it was what I did for a living – I felt out of kilter with the climbing set, and so thought I needed to win some more competitions. Then, still dissatisfied, never pleased with myself, I felt the need to go one step further, if only to justify the money I was being given. I decided to compete in the biggest competitions, with Grenoble and Bercy for starters. At Grenoble, the main poster advertising the challenge showed a photo of me. Everyone was waiting for me... yes, I was ready, I wanted to win. Unfortunately, right at the first climb, I put a foot out of bounds. Disqualified. Never mind. I was a bit disappointed but I had rather it happened right at the start than at the end of the contest – that would have made me even more unhappy.

Not for one second did the organisers imagine that I could be eliminated in the first round. What deal did they come to with their major partner, the City of Grenoble? I do not know, but let it be said that the mayor charged them to intervene so that I could continue, saying that the public had largely attended in order to see me climb and they must not be disappointed – the 'event must be saved.'

The organisers came and humbly asked me to be so kind as to carry on. 'We are in a tight spot as far as the city council is concerned, you have to stay in the competition. We will make a one-off change to the rules, just this once.' I was stupefied that they dared to ask me. What were they doing to the ethics of sport? The pressure that had been brought to bear on them must have been extreme.

By asking me to stay in the competition, they were putting me in a difficult situation. It was unfair from the point of view of the other competitors and yet I was in the spotlight. On the other hand, more selfishly, I was not sure they would alter all the rules, which stipulated that no competitor could take part in the final, unless they had committed no faults in the previous rounds. What would happen if I tied with someone else and it went to a final round? If I were to take part, it would certainly not just be for appearance's sake but because I had every intention of trying to win. Their reply was of course that they would waive the fault altogether.

Despite my misgivings, I ended up agreeing to their request. In taking that decision, I was much influenced by Jeff Lemoine, the technical director of the French Federation of Mountaineering and Climbing and a long-time friend. I trusted him and the arguments he put forward seemed honourable. So I decided to carry on in support of my sport and for the future of competitions and competitors. Grenoble was the first major international climbing competition organised in France. All the media were in attendance: television, radio and the news media. It was therefore important that everything went as well as possible. But for me personally, the decision was disastrous, as by accepting I had definitively cut myself off from other climbers.

In the end, there was a tie. Three of us had finished the climb: Lynn Hill the American, a German, Andrea Eisenhut and me. The organisers told me, 'Catherine, we are really sorry, but you are not allowed to carry on.'

'What do you mean? But you told me that...' the German, in whose interest it was to have me eliminated, would not have me in the final, whereas Lynn did – it did not surprise me – she was keen to compete against me as she wanted to beat me officially.

What a bunch of liars. How could I have been so gullible? They had pulled the wool over my eyes, it was really sickening. I was just a pawn to them. I cried tears of rage. Instead of trusting them, I should have refused from the outset. Why had I been so weak? My anger did not subside, blaming Jeff too for being dishonest with me. It was his job, and not the organisers' to make sure the rules were adhered to. He was compromising his official status. Lothar consoled me; he thought the situation stupid, but wanted to avoid making a scene. When he does fight, he is certainly capable of fighting hard and does not back down. But Jeff was his friend too and I don't think he wanted to implicate him. His attitude suited me. I would not have wanted him to be involved in all this.

The Bercy competition was to take place three weeks later. I had no desire to take part in it, but was swayed into going by my professional conscience. In the final, I climbed so fast that I did not breathe properly and only got two thirds of the way up, gasping with an asthma attack. Lynn Hill beat me.

The truth was that, after Grenoble, all that competition climbing meant to me was my job, and the need to prove to my sponsors that I was worth it. Afterwards, I won some and lost some. I cared little. Competitive climbing had become an obligation and I no longer derived any fun from it. The betrayal at Grenoble had shattered my ambitions. In spite of it all, when I found myself in my childhood adventure playground, the enjoyment returned. 'Look at yourself,' I thought, 'surely you are not going to spend your whole life doing competitions.' My deeper desire was to find a way back to the dreams I had before.

The two last competitions I did took place in the United States, in Snowbird. The first was held in 1989, in an amazing place, on the outside wall of a huge hotel, at an altitude of 3,000 metres, which was owned by Dick Bass, a millionaire who was mad about mountains. He climbed as many peaks as possible, was apparently a formidable businessman and his finest exploit had been to climb Everest at the age of 60. At the time, that made him the oldest person to have set foot upon the highest summit in the world. An enviable record – what will I be like at that age?

The competition was the brainchild of Jeff Lowe, an alpinist famous for his daring ice climbing and his numerous opening of new routes with aid climbing. Everything was remarkably well organised. As soon as we arrived, we handed in our entry forms and were given the competition rules and the timetable for the days ahead – American-style organisation – efficient and reliable. The competitors were treated like kings. I had never before seen such lovely big hotel rooms. From the picture windows, there was an uninterrupted view over the surrounding mountains, even from the bath-tub I felt as if I were outside.

The elite of international climbers were there, including Patrick Edlinger. He was in the same boat as I – a bit envied, in the media spotlight, and so 'the man to beat'. Having him there was a great relief. All the same, I thought his situation was even more difficult than mine, as he had previously made only rare appearances at competitions, so he must have been all the more stressed.

The climbs were marked out on the only windowless wall of the hotel. It was narrow and very high – fifteen storeys – and was decked out with nose-shaped protuberances to add some visual relief. It was not exceptionally ugly, at any rate less so than the hideous, gaudy structure in Grenoble.

As in Grenoble, the event was to pave the way for the future of competitions in the United States, as this was the first one ever organised there. The media were out in force, and so it had attracted major sponsorship.

I was eliminated in the semi-final for having put a hand outside the line marking the width of the climb. Anyone would think that I had done it on purpose. But, having been eliminated, I felt a weight drop from me. Now for a change I would be able to be a spectator at the final.

That evening, together with a few friends, who were also out of the final, I could at last enjoy the luxurious hotel and stay up later than usual. We had a good laugh together, we had already put competing as rivals behind us and we talked about our personal experiences of the last three days. I was sitting next to Claudine Trécourt, a good climber similar in size to me, when suddenly the conversation turned to the battery of tests the Americans put us through. These included taking a measurement of body fat, a pinch test done by measuring the width of the skin behind the upper arm. We burst out laughing; Claudine and I were far and away the most well-covered on the circuit and the two of us had made a big difference to the average.

The next morning at breakfast, as I was tucking into serious quantities of muffins, one of the organisers appeared. 'Catherine, you need to take part in the final. Last night, when we were studying the videos, we realised that you put your hand out of bounds further up than Mari, who is still qualified to be in. You are therefore one of the girls who stays in, and Mari has been eliminated.'

I thought they must be having me on.

'You are joking aren't you?'

'You can discuss it with Jeff Lowe if you want.

I could not believe my ears. How could this rigmarole be happening to me again. It completely floored me. Everyone would be saying that the organisers had engineered things to get me back into the competition. Lynn Hill's boyfriend was obviously furious, as were many of his friends who saw it as a sure thing that Lynn would win this major American competition.

Jeff Lowe was adamant and swept away all objections – the video did not allow any margin of doubt.

With my substantial breakfast weighing heavily, I asked for a delay and was given the start time of eleven thirty. I won the competition, but the victory left a bad taste in my mouth. I am taller than Lynn, which is why I was able to reach a hold with the tips of my fingers that she was unable to stretch to. The people who set the route were good. In the final, we had only been able to get up to four metres and then it was over: we could not reach any more holds. I felt guilty to have won like that. Patrick Erdlinger however won beautifully. He was the only one to reach the top of the climb.

Being embroiled in yet another unfortunate situation convinced me to give up. It was all meaningless. I needed something different – new experiences, sensations, adventures,

freedom and open spaces. I needed to be able to express myself freely, to be independent, to make my own plans and to
be myself. I needed to stop feeling manipulated by the media,
by my so-called career as a professional sportswoman and the
pressure from certain sponsors to look the best.

My resolve was strengthened by how I felt when I went to
see the climbs in America. In fact that trip brought me to understand what my aspirations were. I realised that I deeply
loved being in the countryside and wide open spaces, I loved
climbing in wild places, sleeping outside, far from everything
and that all these let me dream of a completely different life.

I had remembered how it felt to be alone face to face with
the natural rock, alone with my head and my arms and all
senses alert. The game was changing; one now had to climb
and protect oneself, that is to say put in one's own protection.
One needed eyes to search out every nook and cranny, a body
tuned to use every opportunity for rest and a head to analyse
all safety options. It was a very exciting game. All the feelings
I had experienced as an adolescent came flooding back, un-
changed. It was really extraordinary. Unfortunately, my body
no longer responded in the same way. I was not a 'natural'
climber any more. It was only my mind which was able to
gambol freely among cracks, overhangs and rock faces. My
body had been enclosed in a corset of sport climbing, condi-
tioned by competing and it would no longer follow. I could
not re-adapt. I no longer knew how to play the game which
had so captivated me in the beginning. It terrified me to climb
rock faces and put in my own gear. I was no longer able to
trust them and felt as if I were solo climbing. How awful! I
imagined falling to my death with every move. But what a
joy it was to try and tame the rock and adapt my body to it.

That trip around the States was intended to be for taking
photos but must have been a nightmare for my travelling companions: Lothar, Gérard Kosciki, the photographer, and his
girlfriend Marina. What happened was that my whole being
was in revolt; it wanted to run, walk, climb wherever it felt

like being, without any consideration for photos, training or publicity...

The reality was rather different, as the photographer was there for a reason. Every morning I had to get 'dressed up', and then choose a climb according to whether its aesthetic appearance, the light and the colour of the rock matched. I did it but not with good grace. One day in Wyoming, we were at the foot of Devil's Tower, a magnificent mountain. According to legend, an Indian who was being pursued by a bear took refuge at the top, while the bear, in its attempt to reach him, scratched great stripes in the rocks with its claws, thence the astonishing appearance of the tower. It had been decided, for the sake of the photos of course, that Lothar and I would do short sections of several different climbs. It needed to be done quickly, as we were only staying in that magnificent place for one day. So off we went to try a fabulous dihedral. We did one pitch, two pitches, then... hey, it's not far to the top... Lothar, what do you think? Why don't we go up and see what it's like? You must feel like it? Come on, it doesn't look far and we'll be quick. Forgetting Gérard, our poor photographer, we went for it, charging up the last couple of pitches.

Unfortunately the enterprise took longer than anticipated. I found myself crawling in a huge crack full of bird droppings on a completely rotten rock. No chance of putting in an anchor. Such terror and such a smell. I crept forward centimetre by centimetre, thinking all the while of Gérard, who must be getting annoyed with waiting so long. But it had been such a long time since we last had this kind of freedom. In the end we succeeded, filthy, dishevelled and... disappointed, in reaching what turned out to be no more than a pile of pebbles. It's true – I had forgotten that mountain tops are often just gravelly slopes, with the only climax being the view and the satisfaction of being there. Perhaps I had been expecting an Indian to be there, waiting to give me a welcoming reception?

Down in the car park, the reception that Gérard gave us was distinctly chilly. I did understand. He had planned several shots: me doing the splits across the left hand crack, me up-side-down in the right hand crack, me spread-eagled on the face. Images to thrill people…

Nevertheless, our little escapade had been rich in sensations and feelings. I had rediscovered the art of improvising, of un-certainty, of taking risks – in short, of adventure. From that day on, I no longer had any desire at all to pose for photos. I was fed up with the whole circus. I especially felt the need to live, not for others or for the press, not to be acknowledged but just to climb as before – to climb big routes, to see sum-mits, to climb a sequence of faces one after the other. But I was not able to put these desires into practice immediately and I spent nearly a year with a foot in both camps, wondering what the hell I was going to do with my life. The internal strug-gle was not easy and those around me were not much help.

One day, I took the decision that whatever happened, I would follow my instincts. The following year's Snowbird competition would be my last one. I had chosen Snowbird be-cause I like the surroundings and also because I would be able to talk to Jeff Lowe, who wanted me to join him on an expe-dition to the Trango Towers, in the Baltoro range in Pakistan. The aim was to free climb the Yugoslav route on the Nameless Tower, whose summit is over 6,200 metres. He was inviting me, because David Breashers, the famous alpinist and film maker, wanted to film the ascent. If there were a European on the expedition, and what was more, one who was well-known and female, he would be able to obtain funding more easily. Obviously for me, it was a fantastic opportunity to get to know very high mountains with such experienced people.

I came third in the competition. I hardly expected to win it anyway. All that no longer mattered to me. A new page was turning. From then on, I dedicated myself to my passion for mountains, free climbing and adventure.

RETURN TO THE MOUNTAINS
The Trango towers and the Bonatti Pillar

*A passion for mountains is first and foremost
the childhood inside all of us, refusing to die.*

François Mauriac

By way of beginning my new life, while waiting to go on the expedition to Pakistan planned for the following year, I decided to take advantage of the fitness I had achieved over the years of competing in order to do some good free ascents of some really big walls. To me, climbing is a truly formidable game of tactics. I love rock, which I look upon as a living material I have to attempt to tame. Each section has a soul with its secrets and its ruses, every type of rock has its own particular character. Limestone is ravaged, all jumbled up with disorganised contours; gneiss is less so; sandstone is different, being more compact and rounded. As for granite, it is plain, honest and straightforward. Its pure, beautiful consistency is pleasant to the touch and also welcoming due to its colours which are usually in warm, red and ochre tones. Its lines are often pure and slender. Granite is definitely my favourite. When in contact with granite, my body is no longer entirely master of itself. As if it were attracted by a lover, it wants nothing more than to touch and then find a fault or a weakness in order to be able to play with and discover the rock.

Whatever I do, whichever way I climb its faces and peaks, the rock will forever remain true to itself, always strong, always powerful. I will always have to bend myself to its will and its cunning ways. And if I want to stay alive, I need to be wary of it and respect it. When I think of an image of rocks in

87

general, it's a picture of granite shining in the sun which immediately springs to mind. Then I think of myself touching and stroking it. My whole body is warmed by the reverberation of sun on rock. My hands wander gently over the grainy surface. Then my body starts to climb. It is all easy, my movements in motion in an easy sequence, I climb, I climb... a true dream.

In order to attain that degree of physical freedom and that feeling of ease and lightness I decided to climb solo again. I knew that would be the only way I could relive the perfect osmosis with the rocks and go back to an instinctive almost animal way of climbing. I was not prepared to take just anything that came along. First and foremost I needed a peak of nearly perfect shape – the point which children draw for a mountain. It was the Dru which represented that for me; the peak which had nevertheless so disappointed me when I ascended it on that day when I was seventeen. How much training I had suffered, how many rock faces I had climbed in order to dare tackle it one day. And what a disappointment it was! I had not had time to appreciate it: seven hours to reach the top and that was it, not one second to savour the enjoyment. On that day I had vowed to return.

That time I had climbed the American Direct way. For the solo climb I was now intending,the American Direct held no interest. After seeing a rockfall on the day I climbed it, I had frankly no wish to take any unnecessary risks. Furthermore, I wanted something more out in the air, open, and aesthetic. The Bonatti Pillar seemed to fit the bill perfectly. I had never climbed it, and so was delighted to do so for the first time, together with a friend, in order to establish whether the climb would suit me. Everything was perfect, apart from one section: the Austrian fissure.

That narrow crack could not be free climbed, so to get past it, I would need to pull myself up using the pitons which were already there. However these old anchors all looked pretty awful and I did not think I could trust more than half of them.

When climbing solo, I will only put trust in myself, in my hands and strength and in the rock. Who could say whether a piton would hold when it was supporting my weight? This was only one detail: all the rest seemed just what I wanted. As far as the fissure went, I would be bound to think of a way of avoiding taking risks. We would see... I could always use a length of rope to protect myself. In my mind's eye it was all a piece of cake, but the reality would be something else. Ten years without solo climbing, or so very little. Would I be able to do it? Wouldn't I end up stuck and terrified in the key sections? Hadn't these last few years of overprotected and sterile climbing contests put a spanner in the works?

It was August and I thought of going for September, when the mountain is much quieter. With the Dru in a little corner of my mind, I set off to train. All I really needed to do was to climb granite, do some all-terrain work and, most importantly, keep up a decent level of rock climbing. So I set aside the whole month for my training. That was where I was reminded that, in the mountains, it takes more than being good technically. To be an alpinist you also need to be able to feel the mountain and evaluate it; choose a safe route, weigh up the risks of rock fall or avalanches, anticipate how long the climb will take and take the decision to carry on or give up, all these are based on instinct and intuition. But one is not just born with this ability. One needs to spend time in the mountains, observing them, accumulating experience and listening to or reading the accounts of other alpinists. That way, when a new or tricky situation arises, a story or a feeling of déjà-vu can help to take a life-saving decision quickly. That period of getting back my know-how, really reinforced my desire to return to mountain climbing. I enjoyed taking calculated risks.

When September came, I spent my life tuned to the weather forecasts, which were hardly brilliant – the weather was expected to be atrocious. As the days and then the weeks went by, there was no improvement. The Dru got whiter and whiter, and the temperatures lower and lower along with my mood.

As for my motivation... on 15 October, I decided to throw in the towel, to leave Chamonix and move on to something else.

All through the following winter, I could think of nothing but the Dru. I was frustrated and the desire to climb it was gnawing away at me. That peak was becoming an obsession. Each night as I was going to sleep, I climbed it in my imagination, sketching out moves and altering sections. As my imaginings went on, the cracks gradually changed shape, becoming wider and more difficult, the ledges filled with snow, the corners opened and I missed the holds. A real nightmare.

In the spring, the obsession gradually faded away. I was getting ready for the expedition to the Trango Towers with Jeff Lowe. The Yugoslav Route had been opened in 1985 by a team of four climbers, on the south east face of the Nameless Tower. Following a series of cracks all the way to the summit, the natural and logical route they had opened lent itself well to being free climbed. Wolfgang Gullich, the famous German climber, had been the first to do it in 1989 and had given it a grade of 7b. At the time, no one was doing high altitude climbing at such a level of difficulty and Wolfgang's superb performance was hailed by all the specialist press. What was new about our project was that we planned to film the ascent of such a difficult route and, what was more, it would be done by a mixed team of two climbers.

There were nine of us in the expedition as, in addition to the two actor/climbers, Jeff Lowe and myself, there were film crew, alpinists to give technical help with security on the shots on the face and various assistants.

David Breashers, the film maker, would also be holding the camera. It was his idea to film this ascent. He was an excellent climber and alpinist himself who had turned director, making films about mountains to make his passion for them known to a wider audience. The desire to film climbers under extreme conditions had taken him to the summit of Everest, with camera in hand four times, the most recent of these being to make a film in Imax relating the terrible tragedy which happened there in 1996. The film won many prizes at the festivals. Out of the team of Americans, it was David who was the most open to European culture. He was curious by nature and had come to enjoy our cheeses and wines and, to my great delight, had slipped ten kilos of cheese into the luggage for our base camp.

David had an assistant cameraman who did not do any climbing at all. Instead he took footage of scenery, animals, base camp, etc. He was a rather strange chap who used to spend hours meditating, with staring open eyes, sitting cross-legged in front of his tent. The first time I came across him in that position, he scared me witless; I thought he was dead.

Jim, the sound recordist was not a climber either. Like all the people I have known with that job, he was calm and seemed to be living in his own little world. All that the team could say against him was that he snored extremely loudly.

The assistants up on the face, the American Jim Bridwell and the Swiss Lucien Abbe, were completely differing personalities – so much so that it was tricky having the two of them living in the same space. Jim was tall and athletic, with salt and pepper hair, a droopy moustache and a tanned face. He is a star of the rock climbing world. A former hippy, his glory years were in the seventies when he won fame by opening up major routes in the Yosemite in the very early days of free climbing in the United States. In those days, Friends and bolts did not exist, climbers relied on pitons for security. These had to be inserted, often in precarious positions, whilst holding onto the rock with one hand. This technique was so tough that they inserted as few as possible, thus taking great risks when free climbing. Greatly admired for his daring, Jim was and still is the king of rock climbing in Yosemite.

Right from the start of the expedition, Jim seemed to be ignoring Lucien Abbe. In his defence it must be said that they could not actually communicate properly, neither speaking the other's language. I thought this was a shame, as it was at my suggestion that Lucien had come along. I had met him at the hospital in Chamonix, after my fall into the crevasse. He had read about my accident in the papers and very kindly, even though he did not know me, he used to come almost every day to bring me strawberries from his garden in Switzerland, just above Martigny. Lucien, or 'Lulu' to his friends, is not nearly as well known as Jim, but he is also an exceptionally good climber who has opened several very appealing new routes in his area.

I had been able to see him in action during some filming in Mali, where I was the main person in the climbing film. His job was to take charge of the technical crew's security. I had been very impressed by his agility on the rock and had never before seen anyone moving around to attach and remove fixed ropes with such speed on such an unstable surface. The big, bearded guy, with his twinkling eyes had inspired the whole film crew with his prowess on the rock face, so I had thought him the obvious person to join us here.

This was for Lulu, as it was for me, his first expedition to the Himalaya. He was a bit anxious, not knowing how his body would react to the altitude but, when he turned up in Paris with bare feet and with only a canvas holdall which did not even need to be checked in as baggage, I thought he looked happy to be coming along. He pointed out that all the mountaineering gear would be provided by the film producers. Although that was true, I could not help thinking that he was not planning to change his underwear very often, especially as, good Swiss that he was, his bag also contained chocolate, the wherewithal for making a fondue and a piece of speciality dried Grisons meat.

The general assistants were Veronique, David's girlfriend and Kim Lowe, Jeff's brother, who were both in charge of food and supervising the cook and his helpers.

Veronique was very bossy, but pleasant company nonetheless. As her mother was a Parisian, she could speak fluent French. At that time, my English was so limited that, to be honest, I had difficulty following what was being said around me, and so she acted as my interpreter from time to time.

As for Kim, his role was to be in charge of supplies, in particular foodstuffs brought over from the United States, which were mostly intended for eating whilst filming on the rock face and also breakfast cereals. He was not at all a sporty type. Kim was the youngest of eight children, from a family with a father who was so cultured and energetic that he was overbearing. He had not found his way in life and took refuge in alcohol to cope with depression. Jeff had thought that he was doing his brother a good turn by giving him this job. Unfortunately, left to his own devices, he had made some mistakes, for example in his choice of cereals: Rice Krispies, more Rice Krispies and nothing but Rice Krispies. Very light but enormously bulky. At base camp, he did not feel he fitted in and soon returned to the States.

Right from the start of the expedition, there had been problems. Jeff Lowe had money problems linked to the organisation of his last competition in Berkley and had not been able to set off at the same time as the rest of us. We had to wait a whole month for him to join us. The time was well spent in planning the site, in order to be able to start filming as soon as he arrived. We set up the upper base camp, in other words erected tents with stoves at the foot of the face, and then we put ropes up a couloir to get to a platform at the top of which the Yugoslav Route began.

Jeff arrived at last, but bearing bad news – he had sunk the whole of the film's budget in the competition. David paled when he heard this as, while waiting for Jeff, he had advanced enough money to pay all the expedition's immediate bills: hotel, two months' food for fourteen people, vehicle hire, 60 porters' pay, etc. With my limited English, I did not catch all that was being said, but David was certainly far from happy.

Despite the significant money problems, the expedition continued and, only two days after Jeff's arrival, we went up the ropes that had been previously fixed. They followed a narrow ice couloir and it was in that gorge that we had a near disaster. Halfway up, I thought my last hour on this earth had come. We had not set off particularly early and the sun was already warming the top of the rock face overhanging the gorge, making the ice and snow melt, and dislodging some stones which were now hailing straight down on us. We were caught like rats in a trap, with no way out or of protecting ourselves. I was terrified. David and Jeff were very worked up and went into overdrive to escape. I could not follow as my terror had provoked an asthma attack. I did what I could to move forward but, with a twenty kilo backpack, I seemed to be nailed to the spot. I just couldn't do it – it was as if my well-developed survival instinct had abandoned me. All I could do was pray to fate that the showers of stones would spare me as I advanced so very slowly. In the end, we were more frightened than injured and got away with only a few bruises.

When I came out of the couloir, I found David and Jeff engaged in animated discussion. I thought I understood that Jeff was not happy with the approach that Jim Bridwell had chosen to reach this shoulder and I heard his name mentioned several times along with a lot of swearing.

As a result, the next three days were occupied with fixing up a different access which was just ready when Jeff fell ill with a temperature and sore throat. We then spent four days of enforced rest at base camp and the fifth saw us back on the shoulder. We carried a good week's worth of supplies up there. The whole team was present with the exception of Jim who had a stiff neck and also, I suspect, loss of motivation. The expedition was dragging on and the atmosphere within the team was tense. Since the money had disappeared, we were all wondering if we would be paid for our work. Jim's desertion was not a catastrophe as Lucien was there. Even if he was not as well known as Jeff, he was a much stronger and faster climber than the rest of us and would be free to do things his own way.

At last we climbed a few pitches with Lucien fixing ropes

so that David could film down from above us. The action cheered us up but it did not last as we were then stuck for a week on the shoulder due to bad weather; a week of doing nothing, just waiting. I was not particularly optimistic about the outcome of the rest of the project, but managed to remain cheerful. After all, things could have been worse – at the camp we had good tents and sleeping bags, enough food and we were sheltered from rock falls. What more could we want? I was particularly impressed with the attitude of my two companions. David and Jeff did not turn a hair, they just waited. Our patience was rewarded by some good weather and, contrary to all expectation, the face was dry within a morning. Over two full days, switching leads, we climbed the route. The first day, with Lucien's help, David filmed from above. Halfway up the face we set up a bivvy. Sleeping in a pod hanging over the void was a first for me. I was delighted to be trying out this folding platform device and found it to be much more comfortable than lying on rocky ledges which are never completely flat.

All the time we had been at high altitude, I had awoken every night with an asthma attack. I had been told by doctors that I was asthmatic, but thought that was nonsense as, apart from that one time on the climbing wall at the Bercy competition, I had never had any problem breathing. In an attempt to catch up on my sleep, that night I accepted Jeff's offer to try his medication, as he was asthmatic too. The medicine worked like a dream– I had a good night's sleep right through to the morning.

The next day, the weather threatened to get worse, with cirrus clouds appearing on the horizon, so we needed to hurry to have a chance of a successful ascent. We decided that just the three of us – David, Jeff and I would go on alone. The images would not be as elaborate as with our original plan which included Lulu, but we did not have much option. It had to be done this way or not have a film at all, since the American television audiences would not be interested if we did not reach the summit. We needed to return triumphant. David filmed from the fixed rope that the leader attached at the belays.

We reached the summit at dusk. It was snowing. The three of us regrouped ten metres before the very top and David got the camera ready to record our victory for posterity.

'It's rolling,' he said.

Jeff and I moved off one behind the other towards the summit. Only another two metres to go and we would be there... David suddenly shouted out in despair, 'Stop! The camera has jammed.'

Silence. We were only two metres away. It seemed unlikely we could fix it and night was falling. I suggested taking some stills before it got completely dark and that was how our success was immortalised: a photo of us with our arms in the air making a V for victory. Impressive!

Once the photos were done, Jeff radioed down to base camp. That is something else I will always remember. He announced in a monotonous tone, 'I am pleased to tell you that we are at the summit.'

I am sure he was actually pleased but he certainly did not sound it.

The radio response was to ask what he thought about the bad weather that would be arriving in the night.

Without a change of tone, he replied, 'Well, I think we'll just mosey along and abseil down.'

As far as I was concerned, I was not relishing the prospect of abseiling down the mountain in the dark one little bit. My heart was in my boots. It was only Jeff's attitude which reassured me. As for David, he seemed nervous and started talking nineteen to the dozen.

It was presumably a release of tension as the film was now in the bag, but he let out all the resentment he felt against Jeff. The latter, not bothered in the slightest, took charge of operations and we gently began our descent of the 1,000 metre mountain face. We made slow progress but, in comparison with the urgent pace of our ascent to arrive at the summit before nightfall, the gentle rhythm suited us. I had time at last to look around me.

At one point, my gaze was caught by some glimmers of light on the Baltoro glacier, it looked like a town seen from a plane. Quite extraordinary. First of all I thought it might be a base camp but that was impossible due to the number of lights, especially as K2, the second highest mountain in the world which might have attracted that many people, was not in that direction.

I liked the feeling of having people not too far away. It reminded me of when I used to bivouac at Chamonix, alone in my sleeping bag, high above the lights of the town. Nevertheless intrigued by the sight, I pointed out the camp on the glacier to Jeff, who was as surprised and confused as I was at the strange sight. It was David who explained what was causing all the twinkling lights: they were given off by plants or little creatures that absorb the sun's rays.

'Anyway,' he told us 'they will be going out soon.' And just then, one of the 'encampments' started to disappear. I had never heard of this and felt a bit disappointed. The magical vision melted away like snow in the sun leaving us alone in the night once more.

We certainly broke no speed records on that descent but our mood was serene, with never a raised voice, not a single moment of panic; each to his task, looking out for each other to make sure all went well.

There was a big party waiting for us when we reached base camp. An atmosphere of well-being was emanating from the whole team; the tension and irritation that some had been displaying seemed to have evaporated. The expedition had been a success so, with a feeling of mission accomplished and in a hurry to get home, they all set to work packing up. A whole month camping on moraine feels like a long time, especially if you are not part of the climbing team. For my part, I was in no hurry – every detail was new to me on that expedition and being in these mountains, far from civilisation, suited me. Having fulfilled my contract, I felt like simply enjoying this free time.

It had been the first time I had attempted such technical difficulties at high altitude and on such a big face. Thanks to Jeff Lowe and David Breashers I had learned a great deal, especially such things as organising bivouacs on the face, techniques of ascending fixed ropes, choosing gear and clothing. But what had made the greatest impression on me had been Jeff and David's determination. It would have taken a lot to make them give up on the project. At no time, even during the wait in bad weather up on the shoulder, had I seen them lose heart. For them there was no doubt that it was simply a question of being patient. They had seen it all before. In addition, I had been treated to many accounts, sometimes very moving, of their ascents and ones made by other mountaineers, which encouraged and even inspired me in my own life as alpinist. They motivated me the wish to climb great faces, to visit Nepal, Alaska, The Rockies and to have great adventures of my own.

Once back in France, I spent my time planning the project to solo climb the Bonatti pillar in the Dru. All the time we were on the expedition in Pakistan, we had not actually been on the rock more than five or six days, so I needed to work back to my peak performance level. When I climb without a rope, I need to maintain a good safety margin to feel secure, otherwise fear mars my enjoyment.

While I was working on my fitness, I discovered what it is like to have a film maker putting pressure on you. In the spring, just before going to Pakistan, I had been invited to a festival of mountaineering films, where I met Bernard Choquet the director of the film *Gaspard de la Meije*. He was excited to learn of my solo Bonatti Pillar project, and asked if he could film the ascent. To be honest, not only did I not mind, but I thought it an excellent idea. Since I was earning a living through sponsorship, what could be better than a film to help me live off my love of climbing?

I was hardly back from Pakistan, when Bernard called me about it and I had to explain about needing some time before feeling ready for the project. I explained I would need to be in very good physical and mental shape, that the conditions on the face would have to be right and that there should be uninterrupted sunshine.

However, rather than waiting for me to let him know, he called for an update every few days, which began to annoy me. It felt as if he wanted to own part of the adventure, which was supposed to be all mine to lead as I wanted, in my own time without any pressure. I had already seen enough of all that with the competitions. Rather than making me speed up my preparation, his insistent nagging merely made me lose the pleasure it was giving me.

Nevertheless, one fine day I was ready. Bernard was also well and truly ready. All he needed to do was to work out the itinerary, and the day before I was due to go up and bivouac, he suggested I go with him to have a look. With the exception of the day I was airlifted to hospital, I had never been in a helicopter so, conquering my fear, I agreed to go. What a mistake! I was overwhelmed by the appearance of the pillar, which just looked like a sheer, black, featureless cliff – truly horrible. Unable to make out the route I was to take, I waved vaguely sketching out an approximate line on the pillar for Bernard. Once back down in the valley I was beset by doubts; seen from that angle, the pillar terrified me and I could no longer think how I was to climb it solo. I bitterly regretted having gone up in the helicopter and it took me quite a while to get over those feelings and start to feel positive about the plan once more. I managed by concentrating on what I still remembered of it since I had last done an ascent there. In my mind, I went over each section and they all seemed feasible. I focused hard on those positive thoughts until the worrying ones faded away.

On 10 October 1990 I reached the bivouac of the Flammes

de Pierre. There are two ways of reaching the base of the Bonatti Pillar: you can either get there from below by going up a couloir which is exposed to rock falls, or from above from the Flammes de Pierre, abseiling down a few stretches and then quickly crossing the couloir. I preferred to avoid risk taking and so chose the upper access. A friend, Pierre d'Alboy, had kindly offered to come with me as far as the start of the route. I was grateful to him because I was anxious about the ice couloir, not yet being completely at ease with using crampons, and felt that a little security rope would be a welcome boost to my morale.

The film crew came up by helicopter to join us at the bivouac. I would naturally far preferred to have been alone but Bernard thought it would be interesting to film me to see what state of mind I was in just before I started.

He was probably right – it was certainly good for the film, however just at that moment, the last thing on my list of priorities was to talk to him about my feelings. I knew it was not very professional of me, but I could not bring myself to make the effort. All those telephone calls in the previous months had not endeared him to me and I was not very talkative. I just felt perfectly and selfishly fine. My dream was about to become reality. That was all there was to say. I watched a magnificent sunset and then settled down for the night.

Bernard felt let down. He had a great enthusiasm for psychology and he wanted to know what deep urges had prompted me to climb solo.

That night, I slept as I always did, that is to say very well. Obviously, before going to sleep I thought about what the next day would bring, but without apprehension. I was ready. I did not hurry the next morning. In October, the sun does not get round to the pillar before midday and morning temperatures are somewhat chilly; I did not feel like having cold hands. At ten I was all geared up. The sun was shining. Just before setting off, Bernard wished to conduct a last interview. He wanted to talk about death. I could not believe my ears. Not again – this was hardly the moment. I could not help but explode with rage saying I thought he was a morbid voyeur. It was not so much the subject of death, but rather that he was insinuating that I might be suicidal which made me so angry, as if all the discussion we had had over the previous six months had counted for nothing. He just would not let go of the idea that, to climb without safety ropes, one must necessarily be depressive.

At eleven I was at the foot of the route, breathing the intoxicating smell of the granite and ready for action at last. Sitting on the top of a rock sticking out of the ice in order to tie my climbing boot laces with great care, I listened to and breathed in the mountain. My anger had absolutely not affected my state of mind. I remained quite calm and determined.

Finally I got to tackle the rock. With my concentration riveted to the task, I climbed like a machine. Each movement was carefully calculated and weighed up. I did not move a hand or a foot without first ensuring that the other was holding on firmly or placed perfectly. Nothing existed any more beyond rock and climbing movements. My field of vision was restricted to hand and footholds. Without any problems I made my way past tricky sections and my progression on the face accelerated.

From time to time, as I reached a little ledge, I thought I ought to drink but, not feeling thirsty, just carried on. I was enjoying myself. The granite was truly magnificent. Bernard must have been filming me but I was only disturbed once by the noise of the helicopter. On that occasion the din made me need to stop. To rely on my foot holds, I needed to listen to as well as feel the rubber of my climbing boots as they touched the rock. One little grain of sand under the soles can be detected as a tiny crunching sound which alerts to the possibility of slipping. It was in fact then that I became aware of the essential role that the sense of hearing plays in rock climbing.

Two thirds up the route, a little way below the Austrian fissure, I decided to take a break for a snack of some fruit paste and a drink, then I went on up to the base of the dreaded crack. There I took out a piece of rope and some karabiners. Having absolutely no intention of playing with my life by hoisting myself on a single piton, I had decided to go up that section with protection – the rope would allow me some safety using several pitons as runners.

I climbed the wall with ease. The pitons in place were perfect. From now on the difficulties were behind me and I only had to pass a few obstacles before reaching the summit. During that last section I was gladder than ever to be climbing solo. When roped up to a companion, the last few stretches always seem interminable since, despite the easy terrain, we always have to put in protection properly. But here, I was free! No rope, so I could advance at my own speed. Just below the summit, I saw a fabulous chunk of quartz lying in a horizontal crack just next to my right hand. I was allowing myself to become distracted. I decided even so to take it as a souvenir of the Dru and was even more vigilant.

When I was coming towards the summit, voices reached me – the film crew no doubt. Actually, I was quite pleased. Coming out at last onto the platform of the summit, I found the film makers waiting for me, cameras in hand. Pierre d'Alboy was with them too, full of excitement. He rushed to give me a kiss exclaiming, 'Four hours! You took four hours to climb the pillar. That's brilliant!'

He seemed just as pleased as I was to have realised my dream. But the time I had taken on the face was irrelevant – it was not supposed to be a race. All I had wanted was to climb the pillar by myself.

The others seemed tense, they had been hoping to hear my impressions. Unfortunately, all I managed to come out with were banalities such as, 'There were no surprises. It all went according to plan and I wasn't at all scared. It was a pleasure and it was magnificent.' Definitely a bit short and Bernard was not happy. I felt stupid but just could not manage the effort to say anything more.

In the end, he decided to put off the interview until later, back on terra firma, and went off in the helicopter with his crew, whilst I abseiled down with Pierre for company. In the days that followed, there was an unstoppable flow of praise for me from the press.

'After four hours of struggling and dicing with death, Catherine did one last push-up to heave herself over the edge of the summit of the Aiguille du Dru. Her grazed fingers were swollen to twice their normal size. In order to achieve the same thing, Walter Bonatti, carrying a 30 kilo load, had suffered for six days. Today Catherine triumphed without rope or pitons, climbing completely solo with nothing but a pullover and a bottle of water in her tiny backpack.'[1]

Alternatively, 'Walter Bonatti became a legend for his six day climb of the invulnerable face of the Dru... Frenchwoman Destivelle shattered the myth... in four hours.'[2]

This was all being deeply unfair to the Italian climber. The two ascents cannot be compared in any way. In 1956 it was an incredible, if not to say unbelievable challenge to conquer the Dru by this route. Never before had a route of such difficulty, demanding such sustained effort and commitment, been climbed. The west face of the Dru was first conquered by a big team: Lucien Bérardini, Guido Magnone and their companions. It took them two attempts before they succeeded. Bonatti however was alone and the route he chose was steeper and more continuous. His approach to the route was trickier and, most significantly, once committed to the ascent, it became almost impossible to go back down.

To climb the pillar, he had to master the brand new technique of artificial climbing, that is to say putting in piton after piton to forge a way through where there were not enough holds to be able to do it naturally. At the time, that necessitated heavy equipment (pitons, wooden wedges, karabiners, etriers) and complicated moves with the rope. Also, at the time, it was

---

1 Jean-François Chaigneau, *Paris Match*, 25 October 1990.
2 Ibid.

not known to what extent these techniques could be used on Chamonix granite.

Furthermore, for a single climber, the difficulties were multiplied: he had to scale the length of the rope putting in his pitons, using fragile security, then abseil down, go back up to collect the pitons and the karabiners and finally haul his bag up. In all, the itinerary is covered three times: twice going up and once going down. For a 600 metre pillar, that means several days on the face and so equipment for drinking, eating and bivouacking has to be part of the load. Bonatti spent six days up there. Nobody had ever seen anything like that before; even on the sunny faces of the Yosemite in the United States. This was the Dru, on one of the Alps' peaks most liable to storms and tempests and at an altitude of over 3,000 metres.

My ascent was of a totally different nature. I already knew the route and had the advantage of 35 years of technical progress in the sport of rock climbing. What was more, contrary to what the journalists maintained, mine was not the first solo ascent of the pillar; Éric Escoffier and Alain Ghersen, two excellent climbers in the 1980s had done it two or three years before me. I was just the first girl to have done that ascent solo.

I found all the comments inaccurate and unfair. From then on, I began to think that actually, I too would like to attempt to climb a new route by myself.

THE DRU: A FIRST

*The truth, with all this effort, is that
you are climbing for the sake of climbing.*
Jules Michelet
(1798-1874)

At first it was only an idea, a sort of dream. Then in December
Jeff Lowe arrived in France. Since our expedition to the
Trango towers, we had become very close. His finances were
in a parlous state and he had come to get away from it all, taking advantage of a trip paid for by a sports equipment firm
with which he hoped to work. What he was leaving behind
him in the States was the shame of bankruptcy and terrible
debts to lots of people. Over there, they take a dim view of financial problems of that nature. He wanted to spend some time
in Europe to make new business contacts and to climb. In fact
he had a major project in mind: to open a new route on the
North Face of the Eiger climbing alone and in winter. I was
impressed and also encouraged by his ideas and this spurred
me to tell him of my own similar plans. He did not think my
ideas far fetched and straight away we agreed to help each
other reach our goals. My dream would maybe come true one
day...

Jeff's ascent was planned for February 1991 – in two
months' time. Unlike me and despite never having been to the
base of the Eiger, he knew exactly what route he wanted to
open: a completely straight one, right up the middle of the
north face, in a place where no one had yet dared to venture.

The 'Eigerwand' is a mythical face which all alpinists dream
of tackling one day; a gloomy 1,800 metre wall made up of

layers of frequently rotten rock and bands of snow and ice. It is not only the highest mixed face in Europe, but also the most deadly as there are frequent rock falls and the temperatures are fearsome – hence its nickname 'Mordwand', the wall of death. Overlooking Grindelwald in the Bernese Oberland, it has often been a theatre of tragedies reported live by journalists in search of scoops, which is what has made the Eiger so well known. Mountaineers the world over know these stories and all itch to rub up against it: either to take a known route or to be signatory to a new one. Jeff wanted to open his route just to the right of the Japanese route, solo and without bolts – the Japanese had put in 250. Jeff was absolutely convinced that he had the technical ability, as an expert in both ice climbing and aid climbing to do without them. To several alpinists, this project seemed pure folly and everyone was wondering if, as a result of all his debts, he hadn't turned suicidal.

But even if Jeff was in a deep hole, he was certainly not suffering from depression. This was an ascent he had been wanting try for years, and to do it just now was a sort of renaissance for him. He would get his energy back by doing what he was better at than anybody else, thus proving that he was still capable of great things.

As for me, I believed in him. I was sure that if he had had this idea, it was because he still knew what he was doing. He had already got some mixed rock faces under his belt, some perhaps even more formidable than the Eiger. I knew he was sensible and capable of turning back if things turned out really too dangerous.

Catching a whiff of tragedy, a major American magazine *Men's Journal* paid him for an exclusive. That was something at least. Two journalist climbers, known for their mountaineering articles, were sent down to follow events: David Roberts, who had already interviewed me and Jon Krakauer, a photographer and writer who became famous a few years later for his book *Into Thin Air*.

Contrary to all expectations, Jeff did absolutely no training for the whole of January; nor did he prepare any climbing equipment. He only turned his attention to it at the last moment when he realised he had practically nothing ready. He must have been relying on me as I did in fact have everything he could possibly need: stove, sleeping bag, bivvy bag, pitons, krabs... With everything gathered in an enormous bag, we went to Grindelwald on 11 February and thence to the Hotel Kleine Scheidegg, right at the foot of the north face of the Eiger, which is a strategic position for following climbers' progression with a telescope. There we were to meet up with the two journalists, so-called friends of Jeff but who seemed to me, whatever the outcome of the ascent, to be keener on getting a scoop and a lot of money out of it. They ferreted about, avid for details which were none of their business. They asked Jeff about his financial worries and about his relationships both with his wife, from whom he was recently separated, and with me, and about his motives in attempting this ascent...

I had decided to stay there until Jeff set off for the face and we lived together for seven days taken up with action photo shots, on little frozen waterfalls around Grindelwald and with getting his equipment and food supplies in order. What equipment was missing, was made up by Jon Krakauer who lent Jeff: head torch, first aid kit and a pair of jumars.

Jon and David thought that, for an alpinist of his calibre, Jeff was being dreadfully disorganised. It astonished me too that he should be going onto the fearsome mountain without being familiar with his equipment, but it annoyed me that they were pointing it out. I knew Jeff to be conscientious in his actions and that, when the time came, he would be ready. After all, he had so much experience in using all kind of gear, that he probably did not need to try them out beforehand.

On the morning of 19 February, Jon Krakauer and I went with him to the base of the face. As are all solo climbers, he was loaded up like a mule as he would need all the same equipment as a team of two: stove, tent, ropes, pitons... Nevertheless, walking through the thick snow, I thought him astonishingly full of energy. Even though I was only carrying a few bits and pieces, I found it hard to keep up.

At the foot of his route we said our goodbyes. Then, as there was nothing more I could do to help, and I had no wish to wait at the hotel on tenterhooks with the journalists, I went straight to Chamonix.

Four days later, I heard that he was on his way back down; the blade of his ice axe had come loose and he had forgotten to take the little key to tighten it with. In addition, he needed a bigger selection of nuts and pitons. As I had the missing items with me, I went straight back to Grindelwald.

Jeff did not seem disappointed. That trip onto the face had served as a trial run to reorganise his equipment. Two days later I left again, leaving him to concentrate on the final assault.

The next morning, bright and early on 23 February, he attacked the face. Although I was not there, I knew he was giving his all to pull himself up, inch by inch. In the night of the 27th, a violent storm began, unleashing avalanche after avalanche above him right through the night. It was truly hell; his clothes and sleeping bag were soaked and he shivered all night. Nevertheless, he managed to carry on with his ascent the next day. On 1st March, he tackled what he considered to be the crux of his route. David Roberts wrote:

Watching through the telescope, I could gauge how steep the cliff was when I saw him knock loose chunks of snow that fell 40 feet before striking rock again. At one point it took him more than an hour to gain 25 feet. The rock had turned loose and crumbly: stone towers, teetering like gargoyles, sat waiting to collapse at the touch of a boot, and pitons, instead of ringing home as he pounded them, splintered the flakey limestone and refused to hold. Bolts would have been a godsend.

Yet on those pitches, Lowe's brilliance came to the fore. He thought of one particular stretch of 50 feet as a kind of never-never land: it was the crux of the whole route to this

point. A more driven, impatient alpinist might succumb to
dizzy panic at this point, where the slightest misjudgement
could rip protection loose and send him hurtling into the void.
With his phlegmatic disposition, Lowe inched his way
through his never-never land in a cloud of Buddhist calm.[1]

From our having climbed together, I know that, in moments
of great stress, Jeff is very, very strong. The smallest error
could pull out his safety bolts, throwing him into the void, but
in these circumstances he knows how to remain calm and concentrated.

For those who were watching his ascent, Jeff looked as if
he were climbing slowly, whereas in reality he was breaking a
speed record. The route adjacent to his had afforded six Japanese climbers 30 days' hard labour. Not far from there, the
Czech route was opened in 41 days by four alpinists.

On the ninth day, only 100 metres from the summit, Jeff
was picked up by helicopter just before a storm hit. He had
opened his route in a total of thirteen days, having demon-
strated technical brilliance and without losing his nerve.

Naturally, the finest climbers of the day paid homage to his
superb performance. However our French mountaineering
magazines could not headline him, as they were unable to obtain photographs of Jeff in action. Jon refused to release a single image, saying that he had a signed contract which gave him
exclusivity. I thought his attitude appalling. He knew how
much Jeff needed to re-establish his good image in our world
as well as towards mountaineering equipment manufacturers.
An article in specialist European mountaineering magazines
was hardly likely to make sales of *Men's Journal* plummet. It
was no doubt none of my business, but I thought it a shame.

Whatever the outcome, Jeff did succeed in getting a few
contracts with mountaineering-related companies and, a few
weeks later, he returned to the United States.

Now it was my turn to go into action. Initially I had thought

---

1. *Échappatoires*, éditions Guérin, 2001. (*A Mountain of Trouble* by David
Roberts, *Men's Journal*, May 1992)

of going to the Bugaboos in Canada, a magnificent granite range where I was sure to find some lovely lines to open up. But logistically that would have been far from easy.

With the Dru in front of me every day, I found myself taking more and more careful notice of the south-west face. Many lines were already traced upon it, but I had found an as yet uncharted sector. Looking at it through a telescope one day, I detected a narrow fissure cutting upwards through the large, compact, unexplored wall. It ought to be possible to scale that by aid climbing. I was not completely at home with the technique, but the more I thought of that line, the more excited I was. Then there was the idea of learning a new technique which spurred me on.

I decided to open my own route on the Dru. That magnificent peak, as pointed as anyone could wish, presented me with 1,000 metres of granite wall and had the big advantage of being there under my nose. This would be no minor undertaking, but I was prepared to stack all the odds in my favour. I would study which equipment and clothes would be best for the task, carefully plan my lines of attack and, initially, go and join Jeff in the United States, so that he could teach me the techniques of aid climbing.

We went to Utah, amongst the great cliffs of red sandstone that one sees on movies of the Wild West. There we climbed several known routes. My first stretches as leader were memorable. I found it terrifying to pull myself up on protection that I had put in myself. I do not think my mouth was so dry in my whole life.

By the end of a couple of weeks, I began to be more able to trust my anchors as I advanced. In theory, the rule would be never to use bolts. These have a metal sleeve which you drove into a drilled hole in the rock with the aid of a hammer and have a bolt inserted on which a hanger can be fixed so that a karabiner can be passed through it. This is an extremely reliable form of protection on solid rock but has one major disadvantage: they cannot be removed. Jeff would never, ever use them. Ultimately, one might be permitted to put in one or two at an anchor point for reinforcement if there was no alternative. In between these, you make your way by means of removable gear such as pitons and Friends. As in free climbing, there is a scale of grading which has five levels: from A1 to A5. The grades increase as the gear becomes more precarious. This is not exactly physical climbing, it is more like DIY, with tricks of the trade and special knacks of fixing the anchors which sometimes barely hold the weight of the climber, and even then, only if she or he pulls delicately. It is a game which takes its toll on the nerves. I had never before felt as tired after a stretch of 30 or 40 metres.

When climbing like this, you must first and foremost be prepared. If you are suspended from a fragile anchor, the last thing you want to do is make excessive movements. It is best to be able to find the right piton or protection for the job without contortions, so having them neatly arranged means you avoid getting a fright or wasting time. Before a climb, Jeff becomes super-fussy. He does not hesitate to spend the extra time to make sure that each item is correctly stowed in its right place. Then once he has got going on the rock, he is super efficient. As I am a naturally untidy person, I needed to make a big effort to keep my gear properly in order, but it was the price to pay to get on in this new activity.

For my project, I also needed to gain experience of bivouacking suspended on the face. The route I would be taking went straight up a huge vertical wall, several hundreds of metres high. It would be impossible to find a ledge on a slab of compact rock like that and, as I knew that the ascent would take me several days, I would have to find a way of sleeping comfortably while still on the face. The answer was to use a folding platform called a Portaledge.

The first night I spent in one of those hanging stretcher-like contraptions was on Moses Tower, a tower in the middle of the desert. We set it up just outside a giant roof where the drop could not have been more amazing. When I reached the belay station at the lip of the huge overhang, which jutted out twelve metres, Jeff announced, 'We'll sleep here.' I could not believe him. I was overcome by the drop all around us and clutched desperately at the piton from which I was hanging, thinking, 'Surely we can't be going to sleep here. Oh no! There must be a nicer place.' As I looked at the pitons which Jeff had put in. Imagining them coming loose made my blood run cold. The dreadful thoughts made me even more terrified.

Not at all weighed down by the prospect of my awful fate, Jeff cheerfully set about putting up the platform. I tried to help him with one hand, whilst still clutching my piton in desperation with the other one, which meant I was not really much use. It took me a while to get used to the situation. Meanwhile Jeff reached and stretched, utterly confidently on the fixings, to fit together the tubes which made up the frame of the stretcher. It was actually quite easy to erect; the designer had obviously thought it out well. The sections of the pod were linked together with elastic so that it would not be possible to drop a piece.

Once the platform was set up, I immediately felt a great deal better. I could at last put down my feet and sit on a flat surface. How comfortable it was. I now understood why climbers use equipment like this on big rock faces.

From our hanging platform, we had a view of the magnificent sunset. The rays slanting across the plateau highlighted furrows of canyons leading away further than the eye could see. The tower on which we were perched seemed immensely high – rarely have I had such an impression of being able to see so very far. During all my travels, it was only in the United States that I saw similar grandiose scenery. Those canyons, valleys and dried up riverbeds offer an exceptional palette of shades of red and green. I felt quite literally enchanted living in that magnificent setting for a few days. Wide open spaces always act as a tonic for me. They inspire my imagination which then builds grand projects, quite often rather mad dreams...

1989, while filming for 'Solo Thai' in Thailand.

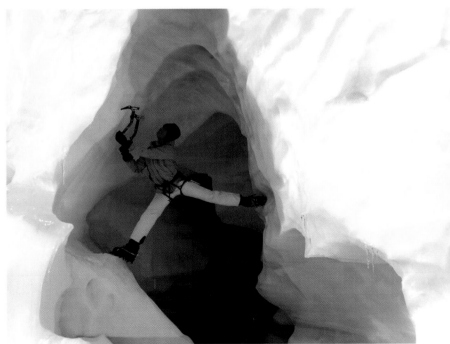

*1992, Training in ice techniques in a crevasse in the Vallée Blanche
before the solo ascent of the Eiger in winter.*

*1992, solo winter ascent of the North Face of the Eiger,
in the exit cracks.*

1994, in Nepal with Erik Decamp on the west pillar of Makalu (8,643 metres)

1996, on the summit of the Nameless Peak (4,160 metres) in the Ellsworth mountains, Antarctica, just before my fall.

2007, filming of Au-delà des cimes (Beyond the Summits): climbing the Aiguille Verte with Lothar and Gaby, 20 metres below the summit.

2007, filming of Au-delà des cimes (Beyond the Summits): top Aiguille du Grépon, with Claire, my little sister. Below on the Grand Capucin, on the key passage of the route 'Voyage selon Gulliver'.

2007, filming of Au-delà des cimes (Beyond the Summits): during a pitch on the Grand Capucin.

I slept wonderfully well. A hanging bivvy like that demands a certain amount of tidiness and organisation. All items of equipment (stove, food bag and everything down to the last teaspoon) need to be hooked on unless you want to risk watching them fly away. Where we were, losing a bowl or any other object would not have been too much of a problem. We could cope for just one night. But up in the mountains, the loss of the slightest object could have dramatic consequences. For example without a lighter one would be unable to melt snow and ice for water – and you do not get far without water.

I would be using a portaledge on the Dru, but not exactly like this one, which was a two-man size and a little too heavy. John Middendorf was going to make a smaller one for me with aluminium tubes and I was going to make a sort of tent to fit the platform to protect me from bad weather. After my experience in the Himalaya, I decided that I did not want nylon – I preferred to use something waterproof but also breathable. The tent in which we had been held up for six days by bad weather at a height of 5,000 metres on the Nameless Tower in Pakistan, was of nylon – it was intolerable as there had been a permanent three to four millimetre coating of frost on the inside – the sleeping bags and clothes were also coated. My ascent of the Dru would take several days and it was highly likely that I would have to experience unpleasant weather conditions and I did not want my mood to be affected by similar inconveniences. Also, to keep cheerful I wanted the material to be brightly coloured: red or yellow. There is nothing more depressing than being stuck in a greenish or greyish shelter.

At the end of the trip, we opened up a new route in the Zion National Park, in Nevada. Jeff, who had stayed there several times, knew the area and its climbers well. He had already marked out different routes. On this occasion I took his advice and decided to wear special boots designed for aid climbing, with rigid soles, a small heel at the back and reinforced tips for better comfort on etriers. These boots have been designed well for that specific use but on rock they are a real nightmare. I was swearing the whole way. From time to time we came across sections which were possible to free climb, but the smooth soles meant that there was no way I could go for it. It felt as if I were wearing clogs. It was intensely frustrating for a free climber to have to continue placing pegs when it would have been so much faster to free climb. Be that as it may, I did manage – I was learning about protection which could useful and I knew that the choice of footwear on the Dru would be my own. As on the Trango Towers, I would be using traditional climbing boots with fleecy linings so that my feet would not get cold.

When I returned to France, reinvigorated by my new experiences, I set about preparing the ascent. This is always a very exciting time when every detail is gone over time and again to stack the chances of success in one's favour. I am not in the habit of announcing my ideas from the rooftops, as I worry that I might then be pushed into doing something I did not really want, as people ask, 'So, when is it happening?' I do not want my pride to get the upper hand. Still, for the Dru I did need to ask several experienced people for their advice. To start with, I went to see André Finot who at the time was the head of research at the outdoor equipment company Lafuma. In his sixties, sporty with a keen gaze, and with 30 years' experience in tents and rucksacks. He understood immediately what I was after.

It was with his assistance that I perfected the tent I was going to take, which was red as he only had that colour material in stock. Although he shared my opinions about bright colours, unfortunately there is no market for them as people prefer dark colours in which they can sleep better.

To allow for cooking inside, we designed vents in the base and at the apex of the tent. In such a small shelter, without air circulation you come up against several problems – due to lack of oxygen, the stove does not work very well and there is a risk of suffocating; also, when the steam from cooking goes on the fabric, everything becomes damp, even with a breathable fabric.

To haul my gear up the face, I would need a special lifting bag, a sort of sailor's bag made of a material which would not rip when scraped against the rock, and with flat straps sewn all along it to secure the weight at the end of the rope and to stop it catching on every bump. Bags like that are rarely used in France, where in any case they are not commercially available. In the United States they are readily available, although I find them too heavy. For the Dru, I was going to have a lot of equipment but still not enough to fill something almost big enough for me to crawl into. André had already had some sewn up in a more reasonable size for other French alpinists, and I only needed to ask for one or two adjustments to make them perfect.

As for my clothes, I would more or less adopt the same principles as I had on the Trango Towers. The best insulator is still air. Climbers have been aware of that for a long time, so to have good insulation, you need to have several layers, which means you can adapt to different levels of cold. Each layer is made of synthetic fibres which insulate better than natural ones like cotton and wool. What happens is that cotton worn next to the skin absorbs and retains moisture from sweat, whereas hollow fibres (Coolmax, Thermax...) wick away the dampness by capillary action. Evaporation or movements of air due to convection take care of the rest. The closer it is to the skin, the better a garment works, so climbers prefer the innermost layers to contain a certain amount of elasticity to mould round the body without restricting movement.

That year Lafuma was branching out into clothing but was not yet up to supplying me with exactly what I wanted. So I went shopping to Vieux Campeur. For the outermost layer, I designed something that Lafuma made up for me. It needed to be waterproof, breathable and easy to move in. The jacket had armholes close to the body, two breast pockets accessible from the outside for stowing energy bars, knives, gloves, an inside pocket for fragile things and a collar which could be pulled up quite high, lined with polar fur to be soft against the neck. At the back of the neck, the jacket could close with elastic to stop snow and rain pouring in. There was a removable hood which followed the head's movements and could be adapted for wear with a helmet. There were no pockets low down as they would have been underneath the harness and impossible to use. The trousers had preformed reinforced knees and some strengthening on the seat as well. Obviously the trousers opened right up so that, whatever position I was in, I could still put them on.

Now, as far as clothes went, I was all kitted out. All that remained was to bet on the weather being warm, by adding a little down-filled jacket. As I was intending to attempt the Dru in May or June, I was not too sure what sort of sleeping bag to take. In the end I went for the heavier option made of synthetic fibres because, at that time of year, if the weather turned bad, there would be more rain than snow. When a down bag gets wet, all its warm, insulating functions are lost and it is difficult to dry, unlike a synthetic filled one.

For all the ironmongery (pitons, nuts, Friends, copperheads, etc.), I decided to use more or less what I had in Utah with Jeff Lowe. Apart from one or two exceptions, all my equipment was made in the United States as it seemed to me to be better finished, more solid and better suited to this kind of ascent. For example, pitons of the same shape and length, could be obtained with a range of blade thicknesses. There was not the same variety of choice in Europe. Friends, which are a bit like sugar tongs for pushing into narrow cracks, were also more practical and less likely to move once put in than their French or Italian equivalents. I only took five bolts.

I went to Michel Béal for the ropes. He had given me my first rope as a present when I was sixteen. He suggested right away that I use a rope with an extra tightly plaited protective sheath which would mean it was more resistant to fraying. He did not manufacture these to sell as they are stiff and so not very pleasant to handle. For what I was planning to do, a less supple rope would be perfect and not tangle so easily.

For my earlier ascent of the Bonatti Pillar, I needed a belay

system. Again, I opted for something American although not
quite ideal, as it would not allow me to come down head first;
if I did anyway, it would not stop me at all; but it was better
than using a device with autoblock knots. If truth be told,
nothing better existed. To make up for the disadvantage, I en-
visaged making a knot on my rope every five metres so that,
if I fell and my anchors held, it would never be by more than
five metres.

People often ask me what I do about going out to relieve
myself when I spend a night on the face. It is a good question.
In the middle of the night or in a storm, when you are comfortably ensconced inside a stretcher suspended above an
abyss hundreds of metres deep, going out is neither easy or
pleasant. What I do, is to use a container with a sealed lid,
like a chamber pot, just as our grandparents did not so very
long ago. I cannot count the number of times I was very glad
to have remembered to bring that wonderful little pot. Unfortunately, to defecate, you have no choice but to go outside, so
it is better to go during the day.

At the same time as organising the practical details, I also
needed to finalise my tactics. Water would be one of the most
important things; almost the key to success. It would be out
of the question to carry eight or nine days' worth of water, as
the minimum liquid required for rehydration and cooking is
two and a half litres per day. The best option would naturally
be to melt ice and snow I could gather from ledges – spring
seemed like the best time to be sure of finding any. Another
good reason for setting off then, was that later, in the summer,
there would be a greater likelihood of storms and the Dru are
known for attracting lightning.

In order to know what to do if caught in a storm, I went to
get advice from the mountain rescue police. They told me that
on no account should I hang my tent in a crack, as the water
running down them conducts electricity. I should also be careful to stay dry inside my tent and especially not to have any-

thing made of metal on me, but should hang it as far from myself as possible. To get the weather forecasts for advance warnings of a storm approaching, I took a walkie-talkie and stayed in contact with the world down below; that is to say with Lothar and his friend Schmello who lived in Chamonix, with a view of the Dru from his windows.

Gradually, as I took advantage of their experience, I gained in confidence. By the time I was about to set off, I could see no reason not to succeed. The last important thing for me to remember throughout the ascent was to be patient. Knowing what I was like, Jeff had thought to warn me, saying that it would be impossible to hurry on that face.

By the middle of May I was ready to leave and had gained a fairly detailed idea of the itinerary to follow and of the difficulties ahead of me. My route would be divided into three sections. The lower portion would, I imagined be relatively easy as the rock was fractured there; the middle one was probably the key to the route as the face there would be very steep and smooth. This section started at around 200 metres from the foot of the route and finished 300 metres higher at the base of an immense arch. I would be able to go up it by means of a narrow vertical crack, but I was not sure whether the little fault continued further up on the third and last section. The latter would not present too much of a problem, as the terrain had some relief. However, I did not yet know whether my route would exit to the left or right of the big arch. My decision would have to be made according to the quality of the rock.

I waited for a month and a half, during which the weather was atrocious without the slightest good weather in sight. As I was a professional climber, I took advantage of the time to organise photographic and film records of my ascent. Now that I felt sure of myself, I felt able to talk about it. This time, having learnt my lessons from my solo ascent of the Bonatti Pillar and Jeff's experience on the Eiger, I was determined that I should choose myself who would do the reporting and that it should be friends who know the mountain. But first and fore-most I had to find the money with which to pay for the heli-copter they would need to do the work.

Dany Sebright, the director of the fashion label for lovely clothes which she had created called Poivre Blanc, supported me financially in my projects, although not enough to cover the costs of filming. I suppose she might have agreed to in-crease the amount but, as I could not see what there would be in it for her, I did not dare ask. Since climbing takes a hard toll on hands, I had the idea of contacting a pharmaceutical company which manufactured hand creams. Rather than ask for money in exchange for a sticker for my clothes, I used my physiotherapy qualifications to suggest I gave them lectures on the damage done to hands while climbing. They thought the idea excellent and immediately gave me some money; un-fortunately not a great deal but, as it was at such short notice, I could not hope for more.

Next, as I like wearing stretchy clothes, I contacted the Lycra department at DuPont in Nemours. The result of barely half an hour's meeting was that I obtained another little bit of the budget – my part of the deal was the logo on my clothes and a photo. Now, getting into my stride, I called Volvic min-eral water, whose marketing director I had already met. He was not too happy that the ascent was to be on rock – hesitating as granite didn't fit the brand image – but accepted a deal in the end. He appreciated mountains and he liked me; I left with a load of stickers. Luck was with me – I had nearly got my budget together.

Then, a few days later, Gérard Bourgoin telephoned me. He was the largest producer of chickens in France. We had met at a dinner with Father Jaouen, well known for his work with young recovering drug addicts. I have no memory of how I came to be there, but remember feeling I did not fit in at the little reception for about twenty somewhat alternative types. I looked round for someone who might be on the same wave-length as me and saw a tall chap in a suit who looked even more out of his depth than I was. He realised we were in the same boat and came over to talk to me. Gérard Bourgoin was there to donate 200 kilos of chickens to the charity.

After that we saw each other several times. If he was coming to Paris, he would sometimes call and ask me out to dinner. He was fascinated by my mountaineering stories which took him outside his own world. For my part, I found his outspokenness entertaining and his tales of business interesting. One day we were walking in the Halles district and he showed me places he had known in the 1960s when working as a butcher's assistant. At fifteen, he used to deliver poultry for his father, a small farmer in the Yonne region. He showed me the café where the butchers' delivery boys got together at four in the morning to drink their little black coffees. The place had barely changed. A street further on, someone called over and asked him for a pallet (in other word a case of chickens). It was 30 years since they had last seen each other; one had grown his father's little enterprise into something which at the time was worth four billion Francs, the other one was still in the same job, but they greeted each other as if nothing had changed. As far as his old chums were concerned, despite his success Gérard was the same person. I was touched by his behaviour. When he called that day, it was just to say hello. Naturally I told him what I was up to and about my project.

'When you are on your little scramble,' he asked 'would you consider wearing a logo for a brand of chickens? We are developing a new line, Chaillotine, and need to match up the business publicity with some sponsorship to identify the slogan with someone and get the press interested.'

I was surprised, and hesitantly replied, 'I hadn't thought of that, but after all why not... I would consider it.

'Right, that's settled then. I'll pay for the helicopter.' And he hung up. It took me a while to get over the conversation.

His offer was certainly generous, but I was not keen on linking myself with a brand of chickens; in any case, I was reluctant to mix business with friendship. Before coming to any definite decision, I resolved to talk it over with a few friends. They too thought the connection a bit weird, but pointed out that, as no one yet knew the brand, I was unlikely to be taken for a chicken. Even less so as in fact it was not actually chickens as such, but ready cooked dishes. So I accepted his offer and contacted my friends, Sylvie Chappaz the photographer and Gilles and Nelly Source the producers, to tell them the good news.

Now that everything was nicely organised, all that remained was to wait for good weather. The following days were taken up with ferrying some of my equipment onto the moraine at the foot of the west face of the Dru. As the start was much lower than for the Bonatti pillar, I had decided to reach the foot of my route by going up the couloir which was infamous for its rock falls, and I was banking on fresh snow to slow or even halt the projectiles.

On 23 June there was an excellent weather forecast, predicting a whole fine week with no significant bad weather anticipated. Together with my friends, I went up to sleep at the foot of the Dru. Early the next morning, four of them: Michel Pellé, Lothar, David Ravanel and Dédé Rhem helped me take my equipment up to the foot of the route, each carrying a relatively light bag for maximum speed up the abominable couloir. While Gilles Source filmed, Sylvie Chappaz was taking stills. There was a party atmosphere that evening at the foot of the Dru. We were all very happy to be there. Well, I was anyway. I was off at last. I saw the ascent as a long journey, telling myself that if I took my time, I would reach my destination.

At four in the morning on 24 June, we went back up the couloir. The snow conditions were ideal; neither too hard nor too soft, and I was in top spirits. I felt strong and determined.

At five, my friends left me alone with my bags at the base of the rock. I felt a bit emotional to see them leaving, but quickly pulled myself together, even feeling a sense of liberation. Here I was at last; it was all coming true. Only waiting as long as it took to get myself organised and then I was off and away on the first pitch. From that moment on, I felt like a robot; moving with extreme precision. Nothing existed for me apart from the rock, the points of protection and my climbing technique. That first pitch was perfect to warm me up and gently get my self-roping technique up to scratch.

My first belay was excellent. Rather than pull the equipment up straight away, I decided to keep going and decide later where to site my bivvy. In fact I was thinking of setting it up at the foot of the face, where my bags were already waiting.

Above the anchor, the face turned out to be absolutely smooth and impossible to climb. I would be obliged to traverse fifteen metres to my left to reach a good set of cracks but the slab I needed to cross turned out to be smooth too, apart from quite a narrow horizontal step which cut right across its width. I was in something of a quandary as to how I should get across the section with no faults whatsoever in which to put natural protection. To my great regret, I could see no alternative but to put in a bolt for protection in the middle of the crossing, as taking unnecessary risks was out of the question. With my hands gripping the little ledge, I took a dash at the crossing, thinking I would easily cover six or seven metres of wall, then take out my etriers in a leisurely fashion to put in the bolt.

Unfortunately I had not taken the weight of my equipment into account, as suddenly, after only three of four metres I had no strength left. Hanging by my hands from the step, I had the unpleasant feeling that my fingers were opening. I scrabbled frantically with my feet, searching with tiptoes for any tiny foothold that might take some of the great weight off my hands, but in vain. I had to think quickly for another way of preventing a dreadful fall into the dihedral. In my despair, I managed to find a final burst of energy with which to free one hand and take a hook and etrier from my harness. *In extremis*, I succeeded in putting it on the edge of the step and gingerly climbing onto it. Balancing on my tiny ladder of straps, I needed several minutes' rest to get my breath back and steady my emotions. Calmed down at last, I started to put in an expansion bolt. I had barely hit three hammer blows on the drill when it broke right across. I was appalled and dumbfounded that a brand new tool could shatter like that. After that first moment of stupefaction, I did not dwell on the hows or whys which would not get me back my precious tool but rather tried to think of a practical way of getting across those fifteen metres without protection.

Crossing using just the strength of my arms to hang from the ledge was utter madness as I had just proved, but to carry on with the help of my hooks seemed the safest way. Over the next five metres it did turn out to be quite easy, taking straightforward steps almost as if I were crocheting with a hook. Then the procedure became trickier as, after ten metres, the ledge sloped gently down and my hooks would no longer hold due to tiny crystals powdering the surface of the granite. The slightest jerky movement risked pulling them off to send me crashing into the dihedral ten metres below, and the further I went, the more awful the drop. My life depended on how well I was able to place the hooks and gently ease my full weight onto them. At times I no longer knew what decision to take – whether to go on or turn back – afraid that the way my legs were trembling with fear might prove my undoing. Nevertheless, as I was nearing my goal, I chose to continue and slowly nibbled away at the remaining distance while trying to clear my mind of all fear in order to stay concentrated. Two and a half hours later, exhausted with stress, I reached the end of the ledge at last.

The next section, just as I had imagined, was a doddle compared to what I had just been through. I quickly climbed a fissure of around 30 metres and then put in my second belay. By now it was two in the afternoon. There was still time for me to climb a third pitch to reach a sort of little platform. From that level, another series of cracks stretched out slightly diagonally to the left. The third pitch, about 45 metres, took a while, but the rock was clean and there was no shortage of protection points.

At four o'clock I fixed my third belay and chose to do no more. That was enough of big scares. I hoped to have some time before nightfall to organise my first bivouac, as I did not find sleeping at the foot of the route a tempting prospect. On the one hand, I wanted to feel as if I had gone up a bit and on the other, if there were any rock falls in the couloir, I was not sure I would be out of their way. When in doubt, I preferred to play it safe, that is to say go back down to fetch my equipment and ascend the rope with jumars, pull up my bags, unfold my platform, put away my equipment, etc.

Eight o'clock. That first day had been very wearing on the nerves and I was very happy to be lying in my stretcher. It was just in time as it was starting to rain. I was disappointed in the weather forecasters who had not mentioned anything like this. I was still very pleased to be there on the face. Despite everything, it was not unpleasant to lie listening to the rain pattering on the tent's fabric, quite the opposite, it was relaxing... With my sleeping bag pulled up to my ears, I did make a call to the valley below. I wanted to know what the weather forecast was: not good, storms from eight o'clock, better tomorrow morning but then rain again in the afternoon. I was not terribly upset by the forecast even if it was not what I had hoped for. There was nothing I could do about it. The ascent would be trickier than expected, but not impossible. In fact I was mentally prepared for the unexpected and ready to take all the time that was needed to succeed.

At nine o'clock I fell into a deep sleep.

In the small hours, at around three or four, I was violently awoken by the crashing of an enormous fall of rocks. Peeping out of one of the little ventilation sleeves, I saw boulders the size of tables thundering down and bouncing against the sides of the couloir where the landslide had just happened. Some of them shattered just next to the place where my bags had been lying at the foot of the route. Seeing that, made me feel thankful for having decided not to bivouac down there. Craning my neck I could just see the patch of snow spattered with stones.

At eight o'clock, I poked my head out of the tent. The rain had developed into hail and things were looking decidedly nasty: water was coursing over the rock and the little ledges were covered in greenish hailstones. The clouds hanging round the mountain made it look as if it were smoking and visibility was no further than three metres. There was no point in getting agitated – I would take my time before thinking about going anywhere.

Half past eight – time for a radio session. The bad weather was set to continue but things would maybe brighten up in the middle of the day. The weather man might not have been forecasting any improvements but I was not disheartened. I was well equipped and needed nothing.

At around ten, I decided to go out anyway to make a bit of headway up the mountain. It felt like winter as I climbed, cleaning the holds of hailstones.

As I had foreseen, the climbing at this level was not particularly difficult. There were some good fissures to allow me to pull myself upwards by jamming hands and feet. So despite the driving rain, I climbed 100 metres that day. At three in the afternoon I was back in my tent, soaked to the skin.

There I spent the rest of the day snug inside my duvet while outside the storm was gathering force. The hail, wind and thunder made an infernal din, but I was still not worried. I was in a safe place and was still much too low down the mountain to be at risk of being struck by lightning.

Nine in the evening – time to get on the radio. No real improvement expected either today or tomorrow.

On the third day, 26 June, there was fog so thick you could cut it with a knife and a light drizzle. This was hardly weather to get excited about, but it was not threatening, so I decided to go out. I was very excited about the line I had chosen which seemed excellent.

So I set off again with my jumars, keen and without apprehension, back to the place I had reached the day before: the foot of a huge, compact and slightly overhanging wall which was the key section of my route. The crack I had seen with the telescope was in fact there, just four metres over to my right, going straight up to the sky. It was impossible to reach it from the small platform on which I was standing; there was a smooth slab of rock in the way. There was no alternative but to abseil down twenty metres or so and then run across the face, my right hand armed with a hook, to try and catch hold of it. After two failed attempts, the plan worked and I put my first piton into the narrow slit.

The place was truly impressive. I was surrounded by emptiness with the wall leaning slightly forward; the rope ten metres below me was no longer touching the rock. Just then, hanging from a piton, the crack seemed so narrow (no more than eight to ten millimetres wide) that it was hard to believe it continued all the way up the wall. I was deeply annoyed by the prospect, having hung a great deal on its being there. It was that crack which made the route attractive – you do not find a 150 metres of fine fissures every day.

However, when I had checked it from a distance, it did seem to go up quite high. No longer sure what to think, I decided to give it a go anyway and never mind if it turned out to be a mistake. At that point, the two sides to my character were in conflict. One was bewailing the fact that I no longer had any bolts on me; with them, there would be no need for debate. The other side was basically quite pleased that things were turning out this way, which was hardly the correct attitude of a proper aid climber and was not what Jeff had taught me. But to play the purist was now easy, having been forced into it when my tool broke, rather than through some courageous choice. There was nothing to write home about.

At two in the afternoon the hail was coming on harder and harder. I had only climbed twenty metres but decided to stop and go back to the little ledge from which I had left, before catching hold of the fissure. There I was, hanging from my pitons, with my heart really in my boots. The empty space was upsetting me and I was frozen with the awful thought of taking a dive if one of my anchors failed, so I was not getting anywhere.

At three in the afternoon I was back in my sleeping bag, absolutely soaked. That day, I had intended to move my bivouac up to the ledge to the left of the crack, in order to be on site at the start of the crucial part of my route, but the flurries of hail put paid to that.

On the fourth day it was raining again when I woke up but, when it briefly brightened around ten o'clock, I took advantage of the improvement to move my bivouac up to the bottom of the crack.

At six in the morning on the fifth day, I woke to absolute silence. Peeping out through the little vent at the top of the tent, I was treated to a landscape covered with white. Ten centimetres of snow smoothed out all the contours and it was still coming down. This was getting silly. It felt more as if I were going camping on the face than climbing.

Radio contact at eight o'clock – no improvement expected. My support team down in the valley were keeping a little diary of events. On that day it read: *28 June , fifth day: woke up to 40 centimetres of snow. Catherine joked, ate and went back to bed.*

But at midday I was back hanging in my etriers. I had decided to tackle these frankly unpleasant conditions and so, ignoring them, I nibbled away at the height metre by metre. Making progress like that was wearing on the nerves. Sometimes my pitons were only set five millimetres into the crack and I was constantly expecting one of them to give. The fall would not be dangerous, as it would be into air without even

135

touching the face. Nevertheless, I really had no desire to fall.

At two in the afternoon I had made only fifteen metres' progress but decided to call it a day. The wet was starting to seep into my clothes and, more importantly, I wanted to look after my hands which were only covered by fingerless gloves. That meant that my fingers were working in direct contact with water, ice and rock. In extreme conditions like this, the fingers swell and the skin bursts open next to the nails, becoming chapped. It is horribly painful and takes a long time to heal. I was hoping to put off the inevitability of this happening. In all the accounts relating to similar climbs this problem seems to happen. I remember an anecdote about the first ascent of the Bonatti Pillar on the Dru: 'When he got back down to the Charpoua Refuge, all the alpinists there welcomed him like a hero. His hands were so damaged that he needed help to unzip his flies.'

Three in the afternoon saw me back in my shelter with all my clothes wet yet again. I settled quickly into my sleeping bag and had some soup to warm me up. The heat of my body would dry my clothes. I was pretty glad to have chosen a synthetic sleeping bag. A traditional down-filled one would already have become useless.

From my tea time radio session, I learned that it was going to get colder but no better.

Apart from the hardly thrilling forecast, it was rather nice to chat with my friends down in the valley. They seemed slightly worried to know I was in the middle of a blizzard and I could not say much more than to reassure them that all was well. I couldn't do anything about the problem except wait it out patiently. To change the subject, I asked what they were doing, but did not dare stay on the radio too long to save the batteries. When the weather is bad and I am on an expedition, I love reading as a way of blocking out the hostile surroundings. Nevertheless, this time I could not get into *La Fée Carabine* by Daniel Pennac. I was day-dreaming, thinking about the rest of the ascent – and the howling storm, relentless outside the tent, was not conducive to concentration, especially as the wind had got much stronger.

When seven o'clock came, I really did not feel like crawling out of my sleeping bag to prepare any food. I gave in to reason – I needed to be in good shape for what was coming, so I treated myself to a good meal of soup, dried meat and mashed potato, cheese and dried fruit.

The 29 June, sixth day: hail until midday, then fine in the valley, the Dru's head shrouded in mist, it can't be seen at all. One in the afternoon, mist lifts. She tackles the long crack up the middle of the overhanging slab at about 3,200 metres. Grade A3 and A4 and covers 50 metres. She has a good night in her hanging teepee.

On 30 June the weather was lovely but very cold. I felt fine and hoped to get the big wall over with that day.

By half past seven, I was already at the last belay getting ready to resume my slow progression up the crack whose end I could still not see.

Two hours later, I had climbed another twenty metres. My fears were confirmed – the crack was closing up more and more and then vanished completely into the rock. I was only advancing now thanks to pitons as thin as razor blades and tiny anchors with points as small as the tines of a fork, which could barely support my weight. My stomach churning with anxiety, I cautiously lifted myself onto each one. If just one of them gave, I would go plunging down a very long way. I preferred not to think about it and nibbled away at another few metres. There were only ten more metres of the closed up crack to climb. If I managed to get across this last chunk, I would have won – I would have succeeded on what I considered to be the crux of my route. Full of hope, I turned my attention once more to my protection.

At eleven o'clock, when I had just placed all my weight on a small peg and, with my arms lifted, was about to put in another just above me, I heard a creak. The realisation that the noise was coming from the point on which I was standing was brutal and my blood ran cold. Powerless and terrified I stared hard at the pro praying that it would not move any further. But I had barely had time to comprehend the danger I was in, when I was violently flung into the abyss and found myself hanging upside down from the rope twelve metres below. The auto-belay had held.

Happy to have got away with nothing worse than a good fright, I was surprised to realise that the incident had in fact done me some good. My stress had evaporated leaving anger in its place – six anchor points had just ripped out – that was two whole hours' work wasted. Very quickly however, the fury gave way to anxiety as I felt I had reached a dead end and could not see a way out of. To continue as I had been, going straight ahead was stupid. And why was I so stubbornly fixated on that plan anyway? I probably just wanted to believe in it, as a few metres further the rock would be completely impervious to my little pitons. I was really missing those bolts, just three would have been enough to get me out of there...

I looked to left and right, desperately trying to think of an answer. There was absolutely no way I would give up. Even if I needed to take a few more days, I did not doubt for one second that I would succeed. One of the first things which came to mind, no doubt born of frustration, was to use my hammer to bash notches in the rock from which to hang my hooks; a solution using brute force and ignorance but obviously completely impractical. In any case, I would hate to damage the rock like that. Next I thought of abseiling down 30 or so metres and running across the face to reach the right hand edge of the wall. From where I was, I could not see what was behind it, but I assumed there would be a crack. But to go back down those few metres which I had gained at so high a cost, hardly filled me with delight, besides which, it was not sticking to the line I had imagined. I would put that option aside, maybe to use as a last resort.

Then, paying more careful attention to the rock around me, I caught sight of another possibility. Over to my left was a sort of shell, about five metres in diameter, stuck to the face with, a tiny crevice at its base which appeared to follow its shape around. With a bit of luck I might be able to insert an extra fine piton there and, by going round it, might succeed in getting past the unclimbable section. The prospect cheered me up immensely and I selected the thinnest piton from my collection; it went in barely halfway and did not look too good, inserted upside down. Pulling on it would mean exerting pressure in the direction it would take to come out. In any case, I had no other option but to give it a go. With my heart in mouth, I let my whole weight hang. Nothing happened. Well, how about that? It does not take much to hold 55 kilos. Now in high spirits and ready to tackle any challenge, I began my slow process of improvisation.

Two hours and three metres further, just as I was putting in a piton, I was violently tilted as the piton supporting the etrier my left foot was in gave way suddenly – the whole shell was working loose. For a few seconds I was frozen in panic and did not dare move. What to do now? First clear my head, in an attempt to gain control of all the whirling thoughts. The stress eased and I was able to think more calmly. There was no choice, I had to carry on. The shell was huge and my tiny pitons were not going to make it fall off. I would just need to insert them more delicately. Then I had a brainwave – to take the pressure off the pitons, I could try to put my feet on the rock itself. That should be technically possible if only I could find the holds. Looking carefully over the rock, I detected a few footholds. They were not big, but they would do. From there on, I advanced carefully, sharing my weight between pitons and footholds. It was very tough going and my calf muscles were soon burning while my head felt as if it were splitting. I was having a serious struggle to retain my concentration which had been sorely put to the test by six hours intense hours of stress.

That way on was towards the left hand side of the shell, whose edge was disintegrating a bit. A small hole between the shell and the face let me insert a Friend. It was excellent. Then, just as I was pulling myself onto it to give my calves a rest, I heard a peculiar clicking beneath me. I was horrified to see from a glance down between my legs that the last five anchors had come out and were sadly dangling on my rope. The pressure of the Friend had forced the shell to lift some more. It felt as if I were living a nightmare.

At the end of my tether, my eyes filling with tears, I looked up to see that I only had another three metres' climb to get out of this. I looked at the rock around me in desperation, feeling extremely sorry for myself. It was grey and crumbly. For a while, I just stayed put, rigid and dazed with fear. Then, gradually getting used to the peril I was in, I pulled myself together enough to take another more constructive look at the rock. One possibility came to mind. I decided to try something which is occasionally used by aid climbers on extremely difficult pitches: lead. It is soft enough to be hit into tiny irregularities in the rock with a hammer, and it is a material which can bear the weight of a man. It is a trick which obviously cannot be used to prevent falls, but one which does allow you to move on from places where no pitons or skyhooks can be placed.

Once I had calmed down enough, I set to the task of tapping lead into a dent in the rock. To support that I connected it to a skyhook from a ledge as my thumbnail; so that my weight would be shared between two points. Once more, with heart pounding, I hauled myself gently up the fragile mountain. It held fast. Now standing on the lowest rungs of my webbing ladders, with my stomach in knots, I hardly dared to move for fear of dislodging my precarious contraption. Having worked out that I might be able to put a skyhook onto a tiny crimper about a metre further up, I really needed to work my way up my ladders if I had any hope of reaching it. So I timidly lifted my left arm in search of a hold.

By a stroke of luck my fingers encountered another small hold, just in the right place to let me step up without jolting onto the top rungs and, at the very end of my reach, to put my hook firmly over the ledge high up to my right. Considering this as a little victory, I perked up. I quickly attached another etrier with a karabiner to the skyhook and got onto it without hesitation. At that level, the face was starting to incline slightly away from me and, when I scanned the rock above, I could make out a few holds here and there. I decided that the best way of covering the remaining few metres was to free climb them. It was a bit daring as I was by now fifteen metres beyond the last good anchor, but it looked possible. Now, with greater concentration than ever, I took my feet out of the etrier rungs and placed them on the grey slab.

I had hardly gone up one metre than there was a tinkling as pitons and krabs went sliding down the length of my rope. That made me freeze on my holds. I stayed there, immobile, my heart beating a wild tattoo and unable to move. After a few seconds, I managed to breathe again and gather my wits. Step by step, I climbed the last metres, clinging for all I was worth to the few holds there were and was at last level with the line I had left ten metres below. Another few metres of good cracks and my feet were at last on a solid ledge.

It was four in the afternoon and the nightmare was coming to an end with my feet on a real step. For that belay, I do not know what got into me, but I frantically put in a whole volley of excellent protection, each more solid than the last. Only three would have sufficed but this desperate need for safety must have been in answer to all the emotion of the previous few hours. I decided to set up my bivvy and wasted no time in descending to dismantle the equipment lower down the face. I got great pleasure in moving my bivouac at last– it was a sign that things were moving on – my project was progressing.

I packed the big bag quickly in readiness for hauling it up, went back up the ropes with ascenders loaded up like a mule with part of my equipment and, from where I was going to sleep, pulled the rest up.

That was hard going, even though the bag did not scrape against the big overhanging wall, as I was tired to the point of exhaustion and I was in agonies due to my chapped hands. They had taken the brunt of the climb and far from protecting them, I had even clumsily hammered a finger; one of the risks of the trade, as they say. As for Bonatti, he had completely crushed a finger. His hammer blows can't have been quite as feeble as mine.

As I was hauling my bag, an Alpine chough came and sat on the ledge next to me. I was deeply moved by the presence of the bird and, to my great surprise, burst into tears. I did not know why I was crying but it was a relief. The bird seemed to symbolise a return to life and encountering it marked the end of a nightmare. From the way it was nodding its head, one could imagine it was sympathising and I cried even harder. I could not stop the flow of tears, though I did not want to anyway. A short while later, I heard a woman's voice calling me across the drop: it was Sylvie. Looking around, I saw her over on the Flammes de Pierre. My throat was so tight, I could not make a sound but waved energetically. It was nice to see her, though it suddenly made me feel very lonely to be here. I gave myself a good talking to, to lift my spirits, as I was at the end of my tether and hauling my equipment was taking forever.

At nine I crawled into my nest at last. The first thing I did was to get out my walkie-talkie to call Lothar, tell him of the progress I had made and to get the weather forecast for the next day. He told me that storms were expected. Then I gave him a brief resume of my long day. It did me good to talk but it also stirred up some deep feelings and I had to fight back the tears. I did not want him to hear me crying like a baby.

I was dog tired that evening and had to force myself to drink and eat; all I wanted to do was sleep and not to touch anything as my hands were so very painful.

1st July, eighth day, my friends wrote: Weather fine, complaining about slightly infected fingers but generally in good spirits. She packs up her stuff and continues the ascent. 1.30pm she reaches a shelf in the snow, has a look at the next section and goes down to fetch her bags and tent, comes back up and pulls the bags up. Now 3pm. After a 15 metre pendulum, she finds a small ledge, sets up on it and, with tired voice says she is fed up, can't eat and is worried about the forecast storm.

That day was actually very tough. I was convinced that I had got past the crux of my route and that error of judgement proved very costly in energy. I came across more very tricky sections and was not prepared for them. I did not have the power of concentration I needed to anticipate problems or think how to resolve them. I just endured them and felt no enthusiasm when I succeeded. I did however manage to cover three pitches. Two took me as far as the base of the left hand pillar of the great arch I had noticed with a telescope. It was a giant vaulted structure, which had separated from the mountain, formed of rocks which were fractured in all directions and had been caused by the collapse of a huge chunk about five metres thick, between its two pillars. The layer revealed by the collapse formed a compact, grey, dusty slab.

The left hand pillar I had reached was made up of unstable boulders, which were too dangerous to climb. The best thing seemed to be to cross the grey slab to the right hand pillar, which was of very good stone. The slab's rock seemed much too crumbly to hope to climb across it. So I put in an anchor as high up as possible in the archway and then descended about fifteen metres to run over the face and catch hold of a protuberance in the middle of the slab. There I found I was in a tricky situation similar to the day before. It utterly exasperated me to be back there, which was absolutely not what I had wanted to go through today. I was not prepared to think; I just wanted to put in protection automatically. Now, clinging on, I needed to snap out of my lethargy if I wanted to continue, as there were another six or seven metres of crumbly rock to cross before reaching the right hand pillar. Once again, it was by dint of fiddling about with hooks on minuscule lumps and bumps and with straps to make them hold in the right direction, that I managed to cross those few metres. It took three hours – three hours of intense and exhausting concentration.

Once at the pillar, I went straight up 40 metres. On that eighth day, I was becoming less and less keen on the techniques of aid climbing. I was finding it tedious, repetitive and slow, with the same actions repeated from morning to night: put in a peg, fasten a webbing ladder to it with a krab, get onto it, put in another peg, and so on and so forth. There was only one thing which varied: how stressful the conditions were depending, on whether the pegs were put in firmly or not. In free climbing, your actions are varied and you move along faster; it is a much more physical test of strength.

The challenge for me in that ascent of the Dru, was of a far more psychological than physical nature. That was why I had been in a foul mood that evening during my radio session. I was fed up with progressing so slowly, with making the same movements, time after time, all day long. Not knowing how long the ascent would take, I had brought along lots of packets of soup and powdered vegetables. Certainly, they do not weigh much, but after a while you get tired of the bland food and I lost my appetite, due also in part to my tiredness. I made myself eat nevertheless, so as not to get weak, since I had been so absorbed by climbing, that I had hardly been eating anything during the long days.

The alarm was set for four o'clock on the ninth day. As on the day before, there was a storm forecast for the afternoon and come what may, I preferred to be prepared and move forwards as much as possible before it broke. It was a painful awakening. My hands were so swollen that I could not bend or flex my fingers. Just moving them caused intolerable pain and there was a yellowish liquid seeping from the wounds. Before doing anything else, I spent an hour massaging them and bandaging them up with sticking plaster. Then I allowed myself a few minutes' daydreaming. There was brilliant sunshine. Down below Chamonix was gently waking up. From my perch, I could make out the sounds from the valley getting louder and, if I looked carefully, I could see a few cars moving about. What a strange feeling it is, to know oneself to be so close to civilisation, yet to feel as if one is living in another world, a world in which vigilance is at stake and where mistakes are not allowed. It occurred to me that what was weighing me down the most was the constant state of concentration. However, I would not have wanted to be doing anything else. I wanted to get this ascent finished.

The seven o'clock forecasts put me in a bad mood, as they confirmed that a storm was coming. Climbing with a sword of Damocles hanging over me was starting to annoy me. I was not sure whether to fold up my tent; if the storm arrived suddenly, it would be reassuring to know that my bivouac was ready and waiting for me to dive into. I would make the decision later, when I saw what the next stage of the climb looked like. Twenty metres higher, I found a most magnificent rock – a great slab of red granite. My spirits rose immediately. The route I wanted to take went straight through the red shield which caps the top part of the Dru.

Some fine pitches of rock climbing awaited. I was full of excitement at the prospect of a bit of free climbing at last as I set to on the magnificent slab but, after only four metres, deception set in. Climbing solo, with all that equipment on my back, I would not be able to take on the slabs without risk. My stubbornness in following this line was absurd. Having run out of sleeve bolts and having no desire to endure any more moments of panic, I would need to resolve to change my itinerary and move slightly at an angle to my right to go alongside the shield. In frustration at having been forced to give up my original plan, I climbed mechanically with my head down. The self belay technique was confining me to a laboured way of climbing which felt as if I had a weight chained to my foot. At that moment I was not much enjoying the experience that I had so looked forward to.

The only thing I did still enjoy was the contact with the rock: its structure, colour, mineral smell, its tiny crystals shining in the sun and stroking the surface. Without really paying attention, I climbed three pitches. At the third belay, all of a sudden, a voice snapped me out of my robotic state.

'Well done Catherine, keep it up.'

I looked around – nobody. I did not think I had imagined it. I am not the type for self congratulation.

'Yoo-hoo! Here, behind you.'

Then I noticed a hang glider in the air just behind me. This situation managed to make me smile. I would never have imagined being visited like that. Giving him a wave, I saw some big, black clouds behind him. I pointed at them and shouted, 'Look at the clouds. What do you think?'

The man turned his head to look and, without replying, went straight down to the valley. Watching him grow distant, I was overcome again by a terrible loneliness. I would have to face the storm alone. Not wasting a minute, and giving myself a good telling off for letting myself be taken by surprise, I started the task of setting up my bivouac at this new level. It was my own stupid fault that, yet again, I was in an urgent rush. My bad mood had made me stop being vigilant. How long had those clouds been there? As my nose had been glued to the rock since the morning, I had no idea. If the storm really burst, my safety would be thanks to the unexpected visitor.

By a stroke of luck, the skies cleared again. That evening in my tent, despite the hastily enforced retreat, the amazing progress I had made during the day soothed my temper. It might not be the route originally planned, but it was not really so bad, and it had the advantage of being quite direct.

3rd July. Observations from the valley: seven o'clock, steely determination despite another fall which caused both ropes to break, she ties knots. Rotten rock, she descends to take another itinerary which is more difficult but cleaner. Bivouac twenty metres below Austrian fissure.

Actually, that day had begun badly. Twenty metres above my bivvy, as I was trying to pendulum to avoid a section of rotten rock, my ropes were sliced by a sliver of rock. Fortunately the damage was not dramatic; it was just the sheath which had been rubbed off a bit but to be sure they were still strong enough, I made a knot at the level of the worn bit. It was not too much of a problem as, when you are climbing alone, the rope does not need to feed through the karabiners in the same way, so knots in the middle do not delay the climber. I was very irritated by the incident and had to descend further than where I had started from, to set off again on a section just to the right, which was harder but the rock was better.

By eleven I had climbed 60 metres and was nearly on the path to the south west pillar of the Dru. There was a magnificent aerial feeling up there. As there were no threatening clouds I felt no anxiety as I took my time looking around and allowing myself a few moments' distraction to listen to the sounds from the valley. I imagined all the people going about their usual business. I almost envied them. Life perched on the rock was beginning to get me down. On this face, I could not make the slightest move without first weighing up the consequences and I was beginning to feel the need to let my mind wander and give my concentration a break.

Now I was at the foot of a pillar of rock, about one and a half metres wide and six metres high, it stood there like an enormous carved ornamental figure, on a small ledge slightly indented into the face. I started to climb it without even thinking, by squeezing into the break between its left flank and the face. The gap was perfect for foot jams and I went up it as easily as if it were a ladder. A few metres up, I put in a good piton for protection but, without pulling on it, continued on my way and then put in a second Friend. To readjust my ropes, I swung from it. Just at that moment, I heard the first protection tumbling down to the bottom of the crack – the pillar was moving. In a panic, I quickly put in another Friend in a fissure miraculously within reach on the face itself. At least if the pillar toppled into the void, it would not take me with it and I started to feel a little more cheerful.

While my heart was slowing back down to a sensible speed, I suddenly heard voices. Leaning over, I could see six mountaineers on the lower third of the Bonatti pillar; their voices sounded Italian. Just my luck! I would now need to be doubly careful that I did not send the pillar down on their heads. I was not quite in line with their route, but one can never tell what will happen when such a large mass of rock comes down. To make sure it did not go toppling over, I had to climb the alcove with legs spread wide. It was exhausting and I came out with burning calf muscles.

Around two, the sky did not look particularly threatening but better safe than sorry... so I went to fetch my things from 80 metres below. Once the bags were brought up, I continued on my ascent. Thirty metres further up, I was very surprised to find myself on the same shelf as one of the Italians. As far as I remembered, the Bonatti route did not come that way. In any case, whether it did or not, it meant I was too close and my line was spoiled. How disappointing. I hate going up itineraries which cross other ones. I consoled myself with the thought that the summit was not far now and so it mattered less.

As for the Italian climber, he seemed delighted to meet me and he congratulated me and wished me all the best. Our exchange was by necessity fairly brief as we were, after all, quite busy. I gathered that there were ten of them on a course, learning to be high altitude mountain guides. I did not really know what to say to him. It had been a while since I had spoken to anyone, but mostly I felt guilty at being on the same ledge as he was. In the hour it took to fetch my equipment and come back up with all my bits and bobs, the Italians went past me.

'*Complimente,*' they each said in turn, shaking my hand.

Embarrassed as I was to be at the same point as them with my camping equipment, that one little word was cheering.

Alone again, I covered a last pitch, scrupulously avoiding

the Bonatti route, to set up my platform right at the foot of the Austrian fissure. I felt a complete idiot in wanting to follow my own route at all costs. To reach where I was now, I could just as well have gone the easiest way; but my pride had prevented me...

At nine o'clock I was tucked into my tent. The storm that was on its way would not be coming this evening. There had been brilliant sunshine all day without a breath of wind and it had been very hot. I had a dry throat and was thirsty for the first time since the start. I felt pleased with myself for having brought five litres of water up from the previous belay. The face had been heated so much by the sunshine, I could barely find ice to make one litre of liquid from depressions in the rock – that would not have been enough to rehydrate me properly as well as make tomorrow's ration.

The forecast was for more storms but, for once, the poor outlook did nothing to dispel my good mood. Whatever the weather, I had not a moment's doubt that tomorrow I would reach the summit, there being only one more serious pitch to climb. This would constitute a crack which curved round to the left of the Austrian fissure, following which there were just some short sections.

The prospect of getting away from what was starting to be a painful struggle gave me back some energy so that, by six in the morning on 4 July, my hands were bandaged, my bags were packed and I was ready to go.

It took six hours of hard labour to negotiate the curved crack. When I exited I was tired out but nevertheless still keen to reach the summit 120 metres above me; all the more so as the face was now less steep and should not present any major problems. I knew it quite well from having soloed it the previous autumn and so hoped to climb fast. Unfortunately that was not taking my enormous bag into account. My friends' commentary:

She struggled to winch up her bag, which keeps catching on the less steep ground, for ten hours. Eleven in the evening: she reaches the terraces of the shoulder of the Dru. It's a victory.

Those last metres were a living hell. The face was indeed less steep but my bag kept getting stuck all over the place. Initially I went back down to fetch it after I had climbed each pitch and then climbed back up with ascenders on the rope winching the bag behind me, only the damned thing would keep sticking every five metres on some protuberance. At first, I just swore a bit but took it in my stride, initially pulling on the rope with all my might to try and stop it sticking. If it would not come, I let it back down to dislodge it, then pulled up very quickly in the hope that it would bounce past the obstacle. Otherwise, I climbed back down to dislodge it myself, then back up to pull some more; until it stuck the next time.

Over the first pitch, I must have gone up and down four or five times. Each time the manoeuvre took ages, which drove me to despair, as the look of the sky told me that I would not be spared a storm and I was not in a good place. By the second pitch, my anxiety had turned me into fury. With no more thoughts for my own safety, I moved in all directions, struggling for a good hour. Eventually, exhausted by my desperate yet fruitless attempts, I stopped. I made myself calm down and realised with a shock that I had been taking risks while at the end of my tether.

The summit was not here yet and the storm was on its way. I got out the radio to warn my friends. That was it for today. Barely had I uttered one word, than I burst out sobbing as I told my tale of woe. But they encouraged me. They were all there at the summit waiting for me. Overwhelmed, I cried all the harder until I was no longer able to speak and hung up.

A few seconds later I heard voices calling to me, 'Catherine, come on, you can do it. Keep going, we are waiting for you. We've got soup!'

The words were like a shot in the arm. Presumably, if they were encouraging me to reach them, they thought the storm would not be too bad. Deciding to trust them, I continued my laborious ascent. It started to hail a short while later. I did not stop to think, but put on waterproof jacket and trousers and carried on, though even more slowly. Suddenly I heard voices again; this time from below me. Jerking my head up, to my great surprise I saw François Damilano, a guide and friend. He was climbing the Bonatti pillar.

'Hello,' he said
'Hello.'

We both smiled, a bit surprised to be meeting there. I had the practical thought that he might help pull my bag.

'You alright?' he asked shyly.

'Fine thank,' I replied without further embellishment.

I did not want to ask him for help, but hoped he would offer. After all, having got myself into this struggle, I would just have to get myself out of it.

He told me that he was with a client. Daylight was beginning to go and we left it there, each returning to their own activity; he to looking after his second and I to manhandling the rope and my bloody heavy bag.

An hour later we were all at about the same level, climbing by the torchlight from headlamps. I was trying not to show I was desperate and battled on. I thought I might just as well leave my burden where it was and go up to the summit with my rucksack, spend the night there with my friends and come back down to fetch it in the morning. But I did not like that idea. I wanted to get this over with, once and for all. I knew that the next day, to come back down this face would be the last thing I would feel like doing. By now, it was hailing harder and harder. Ignoring my painful hands, I pulled for all I was worth on my soaking ropes. My bag was getting heavier and heavier and seemed to be filling up with water. It was a true Calvary.

As I was thrashing about like a maniac on my ascenders, I

suddenly heard a voice asking, 'Do you want us to help you take your bag up?'

It was François standing just next to me; I had not seen him coming. He seemed a bit embarrassed to be asking me. Later on, he said, 'I didn't know whether or not I should help her. Even right near me, I felt she was living some other experience, as if she were elsewhere.'

What a relief. I was not even embarrassed to accept his offer. I just could not go on...

From then on, the three of us climbed the last two pitches together in the storm. I led and François and his client pushed and pulled the bag. Even they seemed to find it very heavy.

At eleven in the evening the storm abated. I came up onto a ledge a little below the summit. There was Gilles Sourice. I fell into his arms light headed and overcome with the emotion of the reunion. The tighter he hugged me the harder I cried, but at last I pulled myself together and together with him, I arrived at the summit, where Michel and Sylvie were waiting for us. Seeing their faces, I could tell how much they too had been sharing in this eleven day adventure. They both seemed very moved to see me and told me just how they felt, which meant a lot to me; I had not been alone. The ascent would become a part of our history. My joy and my struggles were something that they had experienced too. Stupidly, I was too inhibited to allow my tears to flow and I fought them back.

Then François and his climbing partner arrived, having left the bag five metres below. They were soaked too, but delighted. Sylvie and Michel gave us red wine and soup. How good it felt to be there amongst them, as if it were a big party with friends. The sky had now cleared and it was a lovely night. We spent the next two hours chatting about everything and nothing. Among other things, they told me how euphoric they had been a few hours previously; with the storm breaking around them, they were toasting our success, with their hair standing on end due to static electricity in the air. They must have been truly sloshed not to have realised that they could be struck by lightning.

At three in the morning we decided to get some sleep. As I was crawling into my sleeping bag, Michel asked what I was planning to do in the morning.

'If you want, there's room for you in the helicopter. Think about it, you don't need to tell me straight away.'

Before I set off, I had told them that I was resolved to descend under my own steam. What was I to do now? Intellectually I very much still wanted to descend correctly, but on a physical level, my hands were unable to touch anything without causing frightful pain.

That night I hardly slept; I was too tired and too tormented by the decision I needed to take.

Early the next morning, the state of my hands had worsened. They had swollen to three times their usual size and shooting pains in my finger tips made me need to hold my hands up in the air to make it hurt less.

I drank my tea, by holding the bowl between my wrists. However, the arrival of the helicopter with Gérard Bourgouin on board made me forget my sorrows for a while. I had radioed him from the summit at midnight.

He had said, 'I'll bring you strawberries for breakfast tomorrow morning.'

'Yeah, right!' I said, thinking he was joking.

It was not a joke and I thought I must be hallucinating when I saw the big chap, in city clothes and obviously terrified, crawling on hands and knees onto the little ledge where we were standing. I did not know what to make of his arrival. To be honest, everything going on around about seemed a bit beyond me. Since I had reached the summit, I no longer felt in charge of the situation and was happy to let others tell me what to do. Sitting on the edge of a rock, I watched all the people busy around me. Gérard wanted us to be filmed together on the summit of the Dru; those images would only be for use within his company. I bit back some teasing comments when I saw how overwhelmed he looked. Later he admitted to me that he had cried like a child on the way in the helicopter. When he had seen the grandiose setting and how impressive the face I had just climbed was, feelings he had buried deep within him since the death of his son, six months before in an air accident, had come jumbling to the surface.

Perched on our little platform, with 1,000 metres of sheer drop below us, the film crew got to work. Unfortunately, my remarks were very trivial. I talked about the technical difficulties I had encountered, how slow my progress had been, how I managed to get enough water, the problem with my hands and especially the way I had disliked the repetitive movements. As far as my future plans were concerned, because that is what people always ask at the end of an ascent, I was dreaming of taking a nice, hot bath since, without washing for the last eleven days, I had been gently maturing to a state of personal ripeness. I could hardly blame them, as these were certainly legitimate questions and of course I had many other projects, but I was not ready to think about them right then.

When the interviews were over, it was time to think about the descent. My friends were awaiting my decision; one they would support whatever it was. Gérard absolutely insisted I go down with him in the helicopter and it was not hard to persuade me. My hands were hurting terribly, the temptation was too great and my willpower greatly weakened. Yes, of course, if the helicopter had not been there, I would have abseiled down as usual; the pain was not so bad that another three or four hours would have made a difference.

I got a terrible shock on my return to the valley. First of all there were around 100 people waiting for me as I got out of the helicopter. Standing in front to greet me first was the Mayor of Chamonix, Michel Charlet, along with the town band. So I set foot on terra firma to great pomp and circumstance. This was all surreal; I had just spent ten days on my own on an 800 metre rock face on the side of a mountain, then all of a sudden you are in the middle of a party organised in your honour. I felt extremely uncomfortable being the centre of attention, all the more so as I was not proud to arrive by helicopter. But everyone seemed welcoming, emotional and happy to be praising me. Even the photographers and journalists were respectful and apologised for asking questions the minute I got back down on the ground.

A media frenzy burst on the subject of the ascent. One journalist put it in a nutshell: 'Whoever can this Destivelle be, to have succeeded in doing something that everyone else gave up trying long ago?'*

It was true that in France, no one had done an ascent that way for over twenty years. During the 1980s, the trend had been towards speed and linked routes on different summits. My solo climb to open a new route taking several days was seen as a novelty. Besides which, the fact I was female, excited the journalists even more. I had not been expecting such a lot of press interest and coped with it very badly. I did not enjoy being recognised in the street and was also ashamed of the stunt I had pulled to publicise the 'exploit' by coming down in a helicopter.

It was of course very good for my career as an alpinist to have so much publicity, but the advantages were also at the root of some jealousy shown towards me by others, and when they criticised, they did not pull their punches. According to them, I had only done it for fame and fortune. As I cared more about what my peers were saying than the accounts in the press, it both upset and annoyed me that they could think that.

As far as the ascent was concerned, I had done it for myself and no one else. It was my personal challenge and I had wanted to see if I was up to it. As I am a professional mountaineer, I had turned it to my advantage by organising photos and the film.

I could not just live off love for mountains and water. Nevertheless, I had never imagined that, by making it the way I earned a living, I would be changing the nature of my passion. I did know, however, that money and mountains have never

---

* Alain Roux, *Dauphiné libéré*, 6 July 1991.

gone well hand in hand; linking the two is often seen as a mercenary attitude which devalues the conquest as useless. I have always been astonished by the way people hold on to such outmoded Puritanism, retaining such a romantic vision of mountaineering.

The problem is not a recent one, money has been necessary throughout time; but it was less in evidence. Alpinists were either from a class who had the means to do it, or they were financed by the state. I was of course not the first person to have been made famous for making an ascent. Bonatti, Rebuffat, Desmaison, Bonington, Messner, Chouinard – the list is long – were all fêted by the press long before me and after all, some people still hold out against this form of professionalism, although they tolerate it in other sports. It does not particularly please me to wear logos on my clothes but, having gone professional, I either accept it and keep my word, or I do not participate and I stay that way. I do not like doing things by halves. I had decided to live by my passion and I found a way of doing so. If I had not kept my feet firmly planted on the ground, at least as far as money was concerned, would I have been able to take off for the heights? Financial security allows one to bring plans to fruition without having to worry.

In any case, I did not come away from that experience with a clear conscience. They were saying I was a great mountaineer, while I still only thought of myself as a good rock climber. As far as I was concerned, to be a good mountaineer, meant being able to develop in mixed terrain, where a knowledge of ice climbing was also needed. I had always been in awe of ice and snow, which I did not know well and whose climbing techniques I had never mastered, since I had always carefully avoided them. In order to become a real mountaineer, and go forward in my profession, I would need to learn to climb on ice.

SOLO ON THE EIGER IN WINTER

*When your feet refuse to carry you further, you use your
head to ascend. And it's true. This may not be the usual way
round but surely it is better to walk with your head, than to
think with your feet, as so often happens?*
R. Daumal, *Le Mont Analogue*

My secret goal was to make an old dream come true by climbing the North Face of the Eiger following the route taken by Heckmair and his companions. That north face fascinated me; I was only eight or ten when I first heard about it. One summer, when we were on holiday in the Swiss Alps, there was an item in the local press about an accident which had happened. Although at that age I did not read newspapers, my father talked to one of his friends about it when we were having a meal. He quoted some of the comments, including that this very dangerous mountain was probably the deadliest of all. I saw its photograph in the paper, a big, black triangle. My father told me that Eiger means ogre: a killer. All that made a big impression on me.

I learned a little later that, until the 'sixties, half of all climbers to attempt that face had died. Then in 1972, the year I started climbing, I was flicking through a mountaineering book and came upon several photos illustrating the stories of the first attempts on the North Face of the Eiger. One black and white photograph particularly impressed me. It showed a climber hanging at the end of a rope, his body broken in two at the waist and extended by macabre icicles. That tragic accident had taken place on the second attempt on the face, in 1936.

The first attempt had been made by two German climbers,

Max Sedlmayer and Karl Mehringer, the previous year. In five days they had made it half way up the face. On the last day, observers with telescopes saw them heading for a place called 'le Fer à repasser' before some clouds closed around them, hiding them from view. They were never seen alive again. Two weeks later, the pilot of a plane flying near the mountain saw one of them standing frozen stiff on a narrow ledge where they must have spent the night. It was not until twenty years later that the remains of the second climber was found, buried in the ice in the same spot. That place was henceforth known as the Bivouac de la Mort.

In July 1936 the second attempt was made by four climbers: two Bavarians, Kurz and Hinterstoisser and two Austrians, Rainer and Angerer. On the lower part, they did not follow the same line as the previous climbers, going over to the right on easier terrain, before needing to traverse down to the left to link up with the route take by their predecessors.

Hinterstoisser, the best rock climber among them, took the lead on this traverse which has been named after him. Having crossed it, he attached the rope so that his companions could join him. Following that difficult section, they pulled up their rope and continued their ascent. When night came, they took shelter under an overhang. However, observers had noticed that one of the climbers had stayed still for a long time on the Deuxième Névé, and that subsequently, his companions appeared to be helping him along. Could he have been struck by falling rocks? This hypothesis was quickly set aside the next morning, when the climbers were all seen setting off together.

Around nine o'clock a thick mist settled on the upper two thirds of the mountain and observers did not see the climbers again that day. On the following morning they caught sight of them much lower down than expected, just at the top of the Deuxième Névé, where they were making very slow progress. They had not yet reached the Bivouac de la Mort, which was the highest the Germans had reached the year before. Then they were seen coming back down, with one man being helped by the three others. They came slowly down the Deuxième Névé then made a rappel to get across the rocky ridge and reach the bivouac under the overhang. That was where they spent their third night. The weather was deteriorating fast. Nevertheless, Hinterstoisser was seen heading for the traverse, although exhausted and without a fixed rope, he was not able to get over it again. The only option was to abseil down the overhang which was below them.

In the middle of the day, a railwayman managed to make contact with the climbers, by shouting to them through a window in a railway tunnel in that part of the mountain. The rest of the story was told by him. At that point, they were a few pitches above him and all was well. Thinking that they would soon be there, he cleared a little platform on the snow to help them find the spot, and then went back into the tunnel to shelter from the weather and to make some tea. After a while, when the climbers did not show up, he went back outside to see what was happening. He heard desperate shouts and rushed to the funicular's phone to sound the alarm and summon help. Three guides came to the rescue. They went out of the window in the gallery and traversed the face to find Toni Kurz, about 80 metres further away, hanging at the end of a rope. He was begging them to help him. All his companions were dead.

Hinterstoisser had fallen some time in the afternoon, landing at the foot of the mountain and it was probably his fall which caused Angerer to be strangled by the rope. Rainer, who was injured, had frozen to death. The former two climbers were still roped to Kurz, who had rocks and torrents of water falling down on him but the guides were unable to do anything as night was falling. In the morning, Toni was still alive and calling for help. Despite their best efforts, the guides were unable to reach him. He was hanging from the overhang 37 metres above their heads.

'Don't worry, we are going to help you,' they called 'can

you send us down some string for us to pass you rope and pitons so you can abseil?'

Poor Kurz managed to climb with difficulty up between his comrades' bodies to cut as much rope as he could but it was far from enough. The only way to get more rope was to separate the strands of the hemp rope. He could not use his left arm, which was frozen, but with his teeth and good hand, he managed to get 40 metres to send down to the guides. At that point, they realised that the rope they had to send him would not be enough for him to get all the way down to them and so attached another rope to the one Kurz was pulling on as fast as they could. At last the belay was ready and Kurz took forever to descend. He was curling his useless arm around the rope to keep his balance and using his other one to control his speed. When he reached the join in the ropes, the knot would not go thought his krab and it stopped him. All his strength was gone and his attempts to make the knot go through were in vain.

The guides were unable to save him as he was still out of their reach. They were pulling on the rope for all they were worth to stretch it as much as possible to bring Kurz down to them and it worked. Almost. They managed to touch his feet but not catch hold of them. They shouted encouragement, 'Go on, you are nearly there – we'll catch you. Try one more time.'

Kurz fought again to get the knot through the krab. His face was all red and swollen and his expression vacant and the guides realised he was dying. One of them shouted that he should cut the rope, promising he would not go far. But he was finished and unable to move.

'I can't any more. I can't any more,' he groaned and toppled backwards. A few minutes later he was like a broken puppet.

When I had found the photograph of Kurz, I had not wanted to know the details of the tragedy and had not read the story; the image had made a big enough impression by itself. It must be said, that when I was a teenager I read very few, if any stories of mountaineering. The books seemed too tragic and did not fit in with the image I had, or wanted to have, of the mountains. What I liked to look at was photos and their captions. That same book showed a photograph of four tired but delighted alpinists. The caption read: 'from left to right; the Austrians Heinrich Harrer and Fritz Kasparek and the Germans Anderl Heckmair and Ludwig Vörg on their return from the first ascent of the North Face of the Eiger on 24 July 1938.' On the next page was a photograph of the same four dressed in city clothes standing next to Hitler. The caption read: 'This major premier hit the headlines and was quickly adopted by the Nazi regime for propaganda.' I was quite shaken to see this image.

Initially, the Germans and Austrians had made two separate climbing teams. When Heckmair and Vörg started to climb the mountain, two professional Austrian climbers were already on it: Harrer and Kasparek. Harrer had been careful to take with him a swastika flag to put at the summit. He hoped that, by so doing, he would be selected to join the expedition for Nanga Parbat. Heckmair and Vörg were not too keen on that political movement and were not sure how to react to the competition when they caught up with the Austrians on the ice slopes of the Deuxième Névé. Heckmair refused to be burdened by the Austrians, but Vörg was more generous and persuaded his partner that they should all continue together.

They bivouacked at the foot of the rocky ridge, just a little further than the Bivouac de la Mort. The long couloir slanting up to the left is one of the difficulties of the route they climbed first. They came out of it with a long, horizontal traverse, la Traversée des dieux by which they reached l'Araignée. This is a very narrow ice slope which attracts avalanches and falling rocks. It was here that bad weather caught them by surprise. Having managed to come through, they set up their last bivvy at the foot of the cracks leading out of it. The next morning, they left all their equipment behind, the better to climb the last pitches quickly. Despite the storms and Heckmair falling and his crampons slicing Vörg's hand, they got through to the summit at three in the afternoon on the 24 July. They just had time to descend before night fell. At the station of Petite Scheidegg, they were greeted by a waiting crowd who hailed them as 'heros' of the Third Reich. They were displayed as perfect examples of Austro-German co-operation and the triumph of the will. I find it difficult to judge these alpinists who were won over by the regime. Would they have been able to refuse? In theory, for me, those men were above all true mountaineers just as were the subsequent generations whose names are linked with the history of the North Face of the Eiger.

Since 1938, more than twenty new routes have been traced on the Eigerwand, each with its own toll of accidents. The fascination for it is undoubtedly linked to the many tragic stories about the face, and every alpinist dreams of confronting this myth. In fact the mountain excites a combination of attraction and revulsion. It makes one afraid.*

I was certainly afraid of it. What attracted me to the idea was getting to the point even of thinking about it, without being at all afraid. If I was to succeed, I would first and foremost need to familiarise myself with ice and snow and then master the techniques of ice climbing. My real dream was to solo climb the face, in winter and without a pre-determined route – the choice of season was due solely to the fact that it is less dangerous in very cold conditions. A solo winter ascent would not be a first, but it was precisely for that reason that I had the courage to contemplate one. I reasoned that, if others had succeeded before me, I ought to be able to do it too, provided I did some serious preparation beforehand. It is perhaps rather pretentious to think that way but it is how I have always reacted. I went through that thought process unaware that those who had successfully climbed the mountain in the past, were already familiar with the itinerary; had I known, I would

---

* For further reading about the Eiger: Daniel Anker, *Eiger, théâtre du vertige,* Hoebeke, 2000; Chris Bonington, *Deux Siècles d'Histoire de l'Alpinisme,* Delachaux and Niestlé, *1992*; Francis Keenlyside, *Pics et pionniers, historie mondiale de l'apinisme*, Albin Michel, 1976.

probably have been less sure of myself.

The goal seemed attainable, especially as I expected to quickly be able to reach an adequate level of technical competence. All alpinists agree that it is not hard for a good rock climber to master the techniques of climbing on ice, as the moves are less complex than on rock. What was more, I had faith in my ability to anticipate problems and to solve them when they cropped up. So I spent the winter of 1992 getting myself ready and, as I had done for the Dru, I went to see my master in all things to do with ice – Jeff Lowe.

I took my first steps on little, ten metre high waterfalls above the town of Boulder in Colorado. I was intimidated by the smoothness of the ice. When you are at the bottom of a rock, before you even start to climb, your eyes sweep it, looking for holds. With ice there is nothing, not the slightest irregularity to catch the eye. I found that unsettling. One had to 'create' one's own foot and handholds, by putting in crampons and ice axes on which to move up. Other things which scared me included the actual consistency of the ice, from which I could not gauge its strength and the need to rely on one's gear. In short, my first attempts on ice were hardly brilliant. Nonetheless, I liked it. It was a fun, new game for me and took me back to twenty years before when I was discovering rock climbing: I wanted to make progress and found that exciting.

We spent several days at that site and then Jeff suggested we visit the waterfalls of the Canadian Rockies around Banff and Lake Louise. It was one of my dreams to go there. I would get to know what had been the Mecca for ice climbers in the eighties. In the landscape of famous stories of fur trappers and gold diggers, we climbed some grand and famous waterfalls: Whipping Wall, Baugeot Left... I enjoyed discovering these climbs but was unfortunately absolutely incapable of taking the lead, or if I had done, so slowly that Jeff would soon have lost patience. As second, without needing to worry about protection, I could follow almost everywhere. At first, I rather enjoyed being led but soon became frustrated that I could not take turns to lead some pitches. I always prefer leading; there are more thrills in the climbing game and it is more engrossing. Not only do you have to find ways of getting yourself up, but also need to be aware of safety by ensuring that holds and anchors are secure, to anticipate difficulties in each section to protect yourself, you need to manage your energy so as not to find yourself suddenly transfixed with fear, and at the end of your strength in places where you absolutely cannot fall, you need to make careful choices of what protection to use (ice spit, piton, sling…) and exactly where to place it. It is this tactical game of climbing which I am passionate about.

For me, climbing means climbing in the lead or taking turns with a partner, otherwise I do not enjoy it as much. When I am second, I do not feel as if I am doing much or really taking part. I could not say that I actually climbed those magnificent Canadian waterfalls; when I was there, I was playing the wrong role. Before going any further, I would need to learn to lead climb on easier and therefore less steep routes. Not wanting to subject Jeff to my feeble level as a learner, I waited until I was back in Chamonix before going back to practising.

There, it was not a problem to find people who would go out to play with me. It was when climbing with other people who told me they knew what they were doing on ice, that I realised just what an exceptional waterfall climber Jeff was. I had not realised before, having had no one but him to set an example. To watch him, it all seemed natural and easy. Whatever the conditions, difficulty, consistency of ice, gradient… I never once saw him hesitate or get into difficulty. It obviously made my hair stand on end to see the way he only placed a runner every ten metres, if only to imagine myself in his place, but he seemed so very relaxed… Now back in France, I could appreciate what an exceptional teacher I had had.

It would certainly take a very long time to attain a similar level. But that was not what I was aiming for. Most importantly, for the Eiger, I wanted to be comfortable climbing 80 degree slopes and, thanks to Jeff's tuition, I reached that level quickly. I was obviously not running across the ice, but I had confidence in what I was doing. Reassured by my new skills, I went to the mountains more often and climbed small ice pillars and mixed surfaces, to intensify my training. I needed to get my hands on all kinds of terrain in order to store up as much experience as possible under winter conditions. But I did not overdo it, wanting to maintain my enthusiasm. By forcing myself into the mountains on a daily basis, my keenness for the Eiger would probably have fizzled out and, what was more, spoiled the pleasure I was taking from getting myself prepared. As far as this ascent was concerned, it felt as if I were gathering momentum gently, in readiness to go full steam ahead when the time came.

At the end of February I felt ready, both technically and mentally. All that remained was to wait for a gap in the weather to set off and, at eight in the morning on 10 March I was on my way to Grindelwand at last with Jeff for company. The North Face of the Eiger had monopolised my thoughts for a year and I was looking forward to seeing it. How was it looking?

It was not until I was on the cog and rack railway at Kleine Scheidegg that I caught sight of it at last. My heart skipped a beat. From studying all the photos of the mountain so minutely, I had expected it to seem familiar but there it was before me, so dark and imposing that I was overawed. That first impression only lasted a few moments then gradually faded.

When I looked again, more analytically this time, I did manage to make out the route I had chosen; the Heckmair, the original 1938 route, which seemed the least inhuman to me.

As we had the year before, we checked in to the Kleine Scheidegg hotel just at the foot of the mountain. This Victorian style hotel makes a charming base camp, with its creaking floorboards and its walls hung with pale blue and pink fabrics decorated in old-fashioned patterns. By contrast, our welcome from the proprietor, Frau von Allmen, was distinctly chilly. The tall, authoritarian woman in her sixties assumed an air of disapproval from the moment she saw us. Could she have recognised us?

In any case, she barked, 'Where do you think you are going with that?' She was pointing at a rucksack lying at our feet with an ice axe protruding from it.

'Climbing,' we answered, intimidated.

'You are stupid, I don't like mountaineers. You risk your lives needlessly.'

I could not believe my ears – it was none of her business. I had never before heard anything like it. Whatever she thought, she let us in with a lecture on how we were to behave in her establishment.

We spent a good week in that place from another era. The weather was not great and, more significantly, the forecasts were only bad. There was no way I was going to set off up that face when there was a risk of bad weather.

The week went by slowly. I was impatient to be off. While I waited, I spent the first four days putting the finishing touches to my equipment and staring at the mountain through a telescope. In time, I got to know the itinerary like the back of my hand. I decided to follow Jeff's example when he opened his route; so that I would know where I was, at any given time, I would take a photograph of the Eiger with me.

As for the Dru, I had called on some friends to take photos and film at the last minute. This time, all the costs of filming had been taken care of without difficulty, as it was the sponsor, Whirlpool, who had called me. The brand was keen to support 'women of action'. My friends arrived on the fourth day. The team was composed of René Robert, a photographer, Stéphane Deplus, the director, and a cameraman. They were all very outgoing characters.

Now that there were five of us, we felt better able to face up to the disapproval emanating from Frau von Allmen. She really made me feel like a child who is afraid of being told off.

She only seemed to be nice to her regular guests who had been coming to ski every year for two or three decades on the gentle slopes of Grindelwald.

The morning of 8 March the forecast was fairly good for the next few days. There was a gentle breeze blowing from the north and the sky was starting to clear. I decided to familiarise myself with the way up as far as the Hinterstoisser traverse as, if I were to be able to climb the face in one day, I would need to set off at night. On that first part, there being no obvious line to follow nor particular difficulties, it is very easy to get lost.

Furthermore, since Lachenal and Terray had achieved the first repeat of the route in 1952, the traverse had been undertaken with the aid of a fixed rope. I wanted to check it was still there and see what condition it was in, rather than risk it breaking when I was pulling on it. Lachenal and Terray had fixed the rope just in case they needed to go back that way. They did not want to make the same mistake as the young German who had opened that section in 1936.

For my first foray onto the face, Jeff came with me, and so we went up the first 300 metres of steps side by side, nattering away. I was very pleased with my little recce; seen from close to, the face was less intimidating than I had imagined. I was used to feeling like this, as it had happened on previous ascents; but, even though I was expecting it, it came as a pleasant relief.

On the way up, despite the chatting, I was carefully observing the terrain and noting landmarks and the bearing to take, at a slight diagonal to the right, to reach the section called 'the difficult fissure'. One of the things I was especially concerned about was the surface of the snow; I wanted to make sure that there had not been any rock fall. Apart from a few little bits of schist here and there, I saw nothing to worry about.

At the base of the difficult fissure, we roped up. Whenever possible, I will always err on the side of the greatest safety. This section goes up a smooth limestone slab with some small holds worn into it by water and, 30 metres above it is the famous traverse. My plan to come and put in a strong rope turned out to have been a good one; all we found in the guise of a handrail was a mixture of old ropes cobbled together any old how. Climbing solo, I was not prepared to gamble on their strength and to belay myself, for the section would have taken a long time.

The day before I set off had been assigned for checking climbing gear and going over the contents of my bag to make sure it was not too heavy. I was not absolutely sure I would be able to climb the face in a day, as several things could hinder me: finding the right path to take, working out how to cross some sections, not to mention the conditions on the face which could render some sections extremely tricky and force me to slow down and increase my safety precautions. I did not like the idea of having nothing with me in case I needed to spend a winter's night on the mountain, so I decided to take the minimum bivvy gear: an outer bag, a little down jacket, a spare pair of socks, down slippers and mufflers, a tiny stove, two individual sachets of instant soup, two tea bags, a few sugar lumps, an aluminium spoon and a lighter. In addition, the bag contained the essentials of knife, spare gloves, headlamp torch with lithium batteries, energy bars and a big one and a half litre insulated flask containing a hot energy drink.

As far as climbing gear was concerned, I took enough to put in sufficient safety anchors on a section if I needed to, or to be able to descend in case of a problem comprising: two 50 metre ropes, three ice screws, six differently shaped pegs, four Friends, six nuts, a few karabiners, an ascender, a pair of crampons, a few slings, a helmet and three small ice picks, two of which had a hammer head. I took three of them, since I had heard of an ice climber who had got stuck on the middle of a face because he had broken or lost one.

Feeling properly prepared, I went up to spend the night in the station just twenty minutes from my point of attack. Jeff went with me. I was glad he was there, even though I had no doubts about my ability to succeed in what I was setting out to do, I was nervous nevertheless and his presence reassured me. We slept in the funicular railway staff dormitory. It was a far cry from the soft comfort of Frau von Allmen's hotel bedrooms, but it was nice and warm and, almost unheard of in Switzerland, they did not ask us to pay. To be honest, I did not sleep very well that night. Never before had I felt so excited and anxious at the same time. I was a little afraid of the unknown. In order to get the calm, positive mindset I always have, and also to banish my apprehension, I tried to imagine myself climbing solo. That worked, and I managed to relax for a few minutes until my mind started to wander again to imagining la Rampe, l'Araignée, the exit fissure and I was once more worried about the coming adventure. I was actually in the same state of mind as before taking an exam.

At four in the morning, after a light breakfast, we left the railway station. There was a twenty minute level walk as far as the foot of the route and Jeff walked in front. As I walked behind him, I was muttering angrily to myself because it did not feel very cold, but it seemed to be snowing. A few snowflakes drifted into the beam of my headlamp.

Taking the offensive, I asked Jeff what he thought.

'It doesn't look too bad. But still…'

It was up to me to decide whether or not to go. Was this really bad weather? Undoubtedly not but I would still have preferred clear skies. After a few moments of uncertainty, I gave myself the limit of going as far as the Bivouac de la Mort. Once there, I would see what the weather was going to do and if conditions worsened, I would still be able to get down from there easily. As a precaution, I took a radio to keep in touch with Jeff, so that he could give me more accurate updates on the weather.

Just as we were separating, Jeff said, 'Off you go, I have faith in you, you are going to succeed.'

His words made me really happy. It is not that I had doubts, or that I was afraid, but those words gave me extra confidence.

A quick kiss and we separated without uncertainty.

I had no problem going up the steps in the dark and very soon I reached the traverse which I got past without difficulty. Now I was tackling the first stretch of snow, but without hurrying, as the weather did not really seem to be getting much better.

Jeff had given me some advice about the second rocky outcrop, at the time I was studying the mountain with a telescope.

'Look at that place carefully; do you see? There's a tongue of ice going up to the right. Take it and you'll save time by missing out the rock.'

Logically, he was right – ice climbing is much less complicated than climbing on rock wearing crampons but, looking at the vertical section of ice, there was no way I felt like going up it by myself, as I was still uncomfortable with very steep ice. I was more at ease on rock and preferred by far to swing out a few times from the slightly overhanging rock. In the event, getting over the ridge was easy; it took a fair bit of athleticism but the holds were good and strong.

Before long, I was on the Deuxième Névé. I have never much liked walking in the snow and going up this section seemed to take a dreadfully long time. I find the exercise both tiring and tedious, while on more challenging sections, my mind and body ignore the effort, occupied as they are by the game of climbing, and do not balk at hard work over long periods.

Up there on the névé, stupidly putting one foot in front of the other and forcing myself to conserve energy for later, I had time to think of other things; most of all that I was getting fed up with this stretch. Would it never end? I was looking forward to tackling real technical difficulties. I was thirsty; deep down, I knew that I ought to stop and have a drink, but I did not feel like it in the middle of this snow slope. I would drink when I got to the Bivouac de la Mort.

Another thought was nagging at me – the weather. It was still snowing and, rather than encouraging me to go on, the idea that I might have to go back down was making my legs sluggish. Stopping to pant every twenty paces, I finally reached the famous Bivouac de la Mort. Once there, my first action was to check my watch. It was already one in the afternoon. Having had nothing to eat or drink since I set off, I was hardly surprised at the way being hungry had slowed me down and replenishing my energy levels became a priority. As I sat there munching my fruit bars, I could not prevent my thoughts from straying to the two German mountaineers who died of exhaustion at this very spot in 1935. When alpinists are killed in the mountains, people always say, 'He died where he loved to be, it was a good way to die.'

I love to be in the mountains but not for too long. What I like above all else is going back home. To die on a mountain would absolutely not be what I wished for and, even though I do not believe in the hereafter, I would not want my body to stay in such a hostile place.

Snowflakes were still falling here and there but the sky did seem to want to clear. I felt duty bound to call Jeff, who confirmed my impressions; good weather was coming. I now needed to get a move on if I wanted to get past the difficult places before nightfall. Without wasting another minute, I attacked the ramp. So as to be able to use my ropes quickly if needed but to avoid carrying them, I decided to pull them behind me. Jeff had warned that I should not take that section lightly – it was undoubtedly the crux of the route. Feeling good, excited by the coming action and with utmost concentration, I took off my gloves, all the better to grip the holds, and set off.

The first few metres were climbed with such ease that I was almost disappointed but, the higher I went, the more the ramp straightened up giving way to a high, narrow chimney. Now at last the true difficulties became evident and nothing existed for me anymore apart from the hand and foot holds which were hard to use, as they were flat, slightly overhanging and covered with a light dusting of snow. I needed to call on all my technical abilities as I made progress, moving with the precision of a robot. I had just one preoccupation – to stay at the back of the chimney for as long as possible – as outside it was really awe inspiring: to the right, the face was smooth and overhanging, to the left, black rock which disappeared giving way to the abyss. That was why I felt safest wedged deep into the narrow gap.

Nevertheless, two thirds of the way up, I needed another plan; the chimney was narrowing to the point where I could no longer worm myself into it. To keep going, there was only one option: to come out of the bottleneck and climb the left hand wall over the void. It took me several seconds' to get this idea into my head, but once the shock had passed, I managed to work out how I was to take the step out to the left without being terrified. I would use a long sling to attach myself to a piton which was just in front of me. With that minimal safety, I calmly transferred my weight onto my left leg to bring myself level with the wall. From there, all went well; my crampon tips were stable and there were firm handholds to allow me to continue without apprehension. I unclipped the sling and went on.

The higher I went, the less steep the wall became but now it was becoming crumbly, forming what looked like piles of plates. Climbing in terrain like this reminded me of my holidays in Oisans and I liked it – I even found it fun. It made a change from the good granite I had been climbing recently around Chamonix. Actually, I think I was enjoying it basically because I was expecting it. I knew that the rock quality on the North Face of the Eiger was poor and I had prepared for the worst. Where I was, it was not awful, especially as everything was bonded by the ice. The very top of the ramp had deteriorated to just a steep slope of black shale. I wondered how teams secured their ropes properly in those conditions and was rather glad I did not have to worry about it. I was going up the slope like a spider, with my body close to the ground and my arms and legs spread wide to get a better purchase on the unstable ground. This would not be a good time to slip.

I quickly reached the foot of a steep, uninviting section. It looked much too hard for the route to go that way. Over to the right, I noticed a narrow ledge, which made a sort of balcony hanging over the face. I felt myself drawn to it. I groped my way across for about twenty metres until level with a little slightly overhanging wall. A solid crack made it possible to get over but, only too aware of the void behind me, I decided to put in a Friend to which I clipped a sling attached to my harness. Then without hesitation I was able to get over the little overhang in two or three moves, to set foot on the Traversée des Dieux. I now had a view of a great, white, horizontal band 100 metres or so long, at a gradient of about 60 degrees.

Conditions there were far from ideal. There was fresh, unstable snow covering the slope. I chose to go across right in the middle, going forwards step by step, making sure that each foot held steady and using the ice axe in my left hand to keep my balance. Then, after about twenty metres, I changed course and my line curved inexorably upwards. I decided I would rather reach the base of the vertical rock face to hold onto dry rock and so be able to catch myself, if I suddenly slipped. Once I reached the base of the wall, I did feel a lot better and more in control of the situation.

Thirty metres on, I found an old, rusty piton from which hung a rope sling in dreadful condition. I was pleased with my find. It meant first and foremost that other alpinists had been that way. Even though I knew I was going the right way, it was a comforting discovery. The piton would also be useful to hold up the ropes I was pulling behind me in the axis of the traverse and which I feared might suddenly plunge into the void below me and unbalance me. Furthermore, I had the ridiculous idea that, if I fell, the old ring would be better than nothing. Whether ridiculous or not, the thought reassured me and let me carry on, feeling quite relaxed.

Towards the end of the traverse, while I was tackling an awkward section, I began to feel that I was really getting somewhere. At that point, I was quite pleased with myself. Since the beginning, I had got through the difficult sections rather well, had not given myself any frights and, all things considered, had rather enjoyed it. Above all I was not tired. Buoyed up by these positive thoughts, I continued on the Araignée. Luck was with me; the ice was not too hard and let me plant my axes solidly.

However, halfway up the slope, a rather gruesome encounter made me increase my vigilance. Some old bits of skin were poking up out of the ice. What had happened? Actually, I was not really keen for more details but naturally assumed the worst, given the infamous reputation of the face. In the mountains, one does occasionally come across human remains. Once, in 1976, on the glacier at Bans en Oisans, I found myself nose to nose with an old mountaineering boot extended by a tibia and then, just below, I found a few ribs. For all the bone fragments were completely clean, the experience made a deep impression on me. The poor man must have fallen into a crevasse. I learned from the local press two days later that, 50 years earlier, two mountaineers had disappeared in that area.

With heightened concentration, I went past the sinister spot without stopping, trying not to think too much about it as I went up the slope. I was soon at a small snow platform at the foot of a light-coloured projecting rock, which was bisected by a vertical crack and covered with a roof. I decided to have a break there, to have a drink and, as the next section looked serious, I especially wanted to reorganise my gear before going on. I started to coil up my ropes. That proved difficult; I needed to pull hard. They seemed to have snagged 40 metres further down. By dint of brute force I succeeded in pulling free the pink one. As for the other one, there was nothing doing; it was well and truly stuck. I decided to abandon it so as not to waste time, even though I hate leaving things like that behind. The ropes were so that I would be able to go down in case of problems but I no longer really needed them, as the summit was not much further.

While I was conscientiously coiling the rope I had retrieved, the helicopter flew up to my level. The visit felt like a rest break. It seemed as if I were looking at something other than the mountain for the first time since I had set off. Such a small thing helped me relax and renew my concentration in readiness for tackling the rest of the climb. Armed with my ice axes, I went straight into the attack on the vertical crack just above me. However, I had barely gone up a metre when I discovered to my horror that inside the crack was not, as I had thought, ice but soft snow on which my ice axes had no purchase. This unwelcome surprise put me in a quandary – how was I to negotiate the section safely? Several minutes passed as I was unable to decide what my next move should be. In the end and with great difficulty, I wedged my body into the crack and, scrabbling furiously with my feet, got myself up another metre as far as the little roof.

There once more it took me quite a while before I could move but in this case it was different. I knew perfectly well what move would get me past the overhang, I just did not dare do it. The move is called a Dülfer, and it consists of going up by placing the feet flat on the face and pushing both hands outwards on the edges. I did not dare try it with crampons on. I tried concentrating hard, gathering my strength, steeling myself... but to no avail; I just could not make myself move. I was not prepared to gamble with my life. Realising that time was passing, I finally took the perfectly sensible decision to put in a solid peg and tie myself on with a sling; then I crossed the overhang quite easily. I was cross with myself for not having taken that precaution sooner – by hesitating, I had lost precious time. The light was now going and I would need to be careful not to take the wrong way on the rest of the route. Several friends had told me that they had got lost at this level at nightfall; the mistake had cost them a second night on the mountain.

Profiting from their experience and making full use of the remaining daylight, I took careful note of the terrain and a 40 metre traverse over to the left, which I did by the book, took me to a small snow covered platform below the exit fissures. Once there, I looked up and was staggered to see that above me was not a cascade of ice but a large, completely vertical groove formed of two great slabs of polished rock had a light dusting of snow on their reliefs. More than disappointed; the discovery almost floored me. This was going to be far from easy. It was already six o'clock, the night was drawing in. The idea of bivouacking did cross my mind but was instantly rejected as I judged that there was still just about enough light to climb the first ten metres of the groove, which looked to me to be the very steepest part of it. I wasted no time before it got dark, put my headlamp on over my helmet and started climbing up the giant groove.

I climbed without hesitation, spreading arms and legs to push on each side of the dihedral. I rather enjoyed my moves, dictated as they were by the shape of the solid rock. I was afraid of the abyss below me but I was concentrating so hard that I managed to shut it out of my thoughts. As I had anticipated, after fifteen metres, the gradient reduced a bit and there were better holds. However, I now needed to switch on the torch. The darkness bothered me to the extent that I found myself gripping the holds twice as hard as normal as I climbed the remaining two or three metres of the chimney. At last I reached a small snowy ledge. There was no longer any need to hurry as it was now dark. I would get there when I got there. So, before starting the rest of the climb, I had a drink and ate a few energy bars while trying to see what was above by sweeping the beam of my torch across the face. It was no use; I could see no further than two metres, which was just far enough to work out that the part of the face just in front of me was less steep and that the tips of rock, poking out of the fresh snow, did not look to be very solid.

I thought again of bivouacking but it was risky; it was too cold. Although I did have an overbag and extra socks, I did not see how I was going to unpack my paraphernalia on this little step. If I waited for daylight sitting upright or standing, dehydrated as I was, my fingers and toes risked freezing or, come the morning, I would be too dazed and sluggish with cold to leave. It was better to move on; even if it meant climbing all night.

Feeling that I was already getting cold I left immediately. The route to follow was not complicated; straight on up to the top. Now, lighting up the relief within a circumference of a metre, I lifted myself up, step by step. I left no room for uncertainty, systematically checking each hand hold and each foot hold. Each move was made with the utmost concentration.

Some metres higher, I realised that I was starting to lose feeling in my fingertips. This was the first time my hands had been cold since the Bivouac de la Mort, so I made myself stop, even though I did not want to interrupt the steady progress I was making. At the expense of the cold now biting them viciously, I got some feeling back into my fingers and then conscientiously went on with my ascent. Another few metres further, I realised that my concentration was fading. It was hard work constantly checking all my holds; besides which my fingers were going numb again. Tiredness was beginning to set in. Once again, I needed a stop to warm up my extremities and give my mind a bit of a break too.

Although it cost me to do it, if I wanted to get off this mountain in one piece, I would need to take care of myself and listen to my body. I was not prepared to take the risk of dodgy holds and there was no way this ascent was going to cost me a finger, so I took a pair of nice, warm gloves from my bag. My fingertips started to feel better almost immediately and, within a few minutes, my fingers were moving properly again. Unfortunately, the climb was too tricky to do with big, padded gloves on, so regretfully I had to stow them back into the breast pocket of my jacket, ready for the next stop, and continue my painful climb in the dark. But five minutes later, I had to do the same thing all over again.

By mischance, I fumbled and one of the gloves went diving down into the black below. I drowned in a surge of adrenaline as I imagined myself doing the same thing and my throat was so tight, the normal swear word would not even come out. After a few seconds, I managed to pull myself together. Putting on the other pair I had been wearing before, I warmed myself up and went on. At least the incident had the advantage of interrupting my little routine and thus making me more careful, so I managed to climb several more metres without tiring. I thought about my parents as I climbed, although I did not drop my vigilance. If they could see me now, climbing solo in the middle of the night on this ghastly rock, they would certainly not be happy. They have always trusted me, knowing that I am careful, but since I opened the new route on the Dru, they have started to worry. My mother said to me one day, 'If they are talking about you in the papers, it must mean you are doing difficult and dangerous things.'

I tried to explain that if I did things like that, it was only once I considered myself up to it and it did not feel at all as if I was taking risks. The media talked about it because I wanted them to, and because these ascents had the reputation of being challenging.

On the North Face of the Eiger, until now, I had mastered all the different sections and, with the exception of the slight hesitation at the overhanging crack, precisely because of my prudence, the ascent so far had been problem free.

Now I was continuing in the dark but even here I was not leaving my fate to chance as each movement was calculated and considered carefully. Albeit extremely tiring, this behaviour was because I valued my life. I was in no way in a desperate plight. So as not to take any risks, I was practically inching up the face.

It took a ridiculous length of time to climb the next 50 metres. I could feel exhaustion setting in. The worst part was keeping up my concentration. After each metre I stopped, I tried to relax a little and then went on. It was a permanent struggle with myself; I needed to be sensible. The temptation to throw caution to the winds and power on up to the summit was great, even if it did mean being foolish or risking losing my fingers.

For encouragement, I talked to myself, 'Come on, stop now, warm up your fingers. There, that's better, now for another metre, carefully...' In retrospect, talking like that may seem peculiar but, while in action, the words helped me keep my concentration.

I reached the final ice slope in the end. I was so glad at last to be able to put on my gloves and now, perked up by the nearness of the summit and armed with my ice axes, I attacked the last steep section with greater cheer. No longer needing to worry about the solidity of every point on which I put my weight, released a lot of the tension and I was able to climb fairly quickly with flowing moves. Unfortunately, twenty metres higher it was all too much and I had to stop: I needed to catch my breath. After 30 seconds, I was off again. A few moves higher, another stop. Looking up obstinately in an attempt to glimpse the summit, all I could make out was blackness. It was pretty discouraging. I could not see how much longer the slope was.

At that point I realised I would need to recover by thinking about my movements again; concentrating on myself, rather than reaching the summit. Climbing slowly, I would be bound to get there sooner or later. With greater determination and with my eyes fixed on no more than a metre away, I set off again. Moving at this slow speed, my thoughts drifted to what came next, that's to say what I would do once I reached the summit. Jeff had promised to meet me there but, in view of the awful weather that morning, I doubted he would. There was no question of sleeping up there – it was much too cold. I would have to go back down in the dark. It would not be easy but it was far better than keeping still...

Lost in thought, I suddenly noticed that I was practically crawling on a slope which was so gentle that I could walk on it normally. As I realised how funny that was, footprints appeared in the circle of light just under my nose. They led off to the right, while in front of me there was nothing left to climb, just complete blackness. I was on the ridge of the summit. It was good to be there at last and the footprints were especially welcome. If I followed them, assuming they did not disappear, it might not be too hard to get down. What amazes me now is that not for one second did I wonder whose footprints they were, as there were no climbers ahead of me. The thought that all I needed to do was follow them, was enough.

Happy to leave the difficulties, it was a delight to be walking upright at last. I was however still careful on the very narrow track. This was not the time for losing one's balance – there was a vast black hole on either side. I felt light and astonishingly full of energy. After walking for about five minutes, sweeping the ground in front of me with my headlamp beam, I suddenly saw a sleeping bag spread out on a small platform which someone had cleared in the snow just to the left of the ridge. There did not seem to be anyone in it. Thinking how nice this was but a bit surprised, I called,

'Jeff! Jeff, are you there?'

The sleeping bag wriggled and Jeff's head popped out, his face bleary with sleep.

'Catherine! You did it!'

And we fell into each other's arms, quite overcome I could not help shedding a few tears. The nervous tension that had built up throughout that long day seemed to come out all of a sudden. I was so happy that he was there.

He said, 'I was a bit worried; I thought you might have decided to bivvy on the face. I was going to come and find you as soon as it got light as I think you would have been frozen. But it's great – here you are.'

'I'm not a complete idiot.'

'I know, I know, I'm proud of you. I knew you could do it. What amazes me is how quickly you learn. It all just soaks in.'

He got out the stove and a bowl to make some soup. While

we waited, we discussed the route, the bad weather at the beginning which had slightly put me off, the awkward sections, and the condition of the rock. He knew just what problems I would have encountered and asked what I had done to solve them.

After a while, Jeff pointed out that we had better tell the others that I had arrived, as they must be worrying. Actually, I had almost forgotten them. He took his radio and announced that it was now ten o'clock and I had taken precisely seventeen hours to climb the face, then he passed it to me. They all seemed very happy to get the news and asked if it wasn't terribly cold up there. It must have been between -10°C and -15°C but there was no wind. All was well.

They told me they would come up in the morning by helicopter, to get pictures on the summit.

When the radio session was over, Jeff brought me a sleeping bag. In his concern for me, although he had not actually lost sleep over it, he had in fact put one duvet inside another for extra warmth. I took off my boots, put on my extra socks and climbed in, so as not to get chilled.

How good it felt to drink something hot at last and relax. We sat in our sleeping bags drinking the soup and talking about our experiences for another hour or two. He told me how, the previous winter, he was in dire straits as he finished his route and had left behind his rucksack, which he now hoped finally to pick up when we left in the morning.

'That way, I'll be able to get my glasses, and also give you your gear back.'

At around midnight, as we finally lay down, I felt as if I were on a small cloud. I had succeeded and reckoned I had done well and without any big scares. All the good memories eclipsed the few difficult moments. Full of contentment, snug and warm in my sleeping bag, my thoughts drifted to the next day and I wondered what I would like to do when I got down off the mountain. After careful consideration, I decided that I wanted to eat some excellent Swiss chocolate profiteroles.

With my mouth watering, I fell into the deep sleep of the just. It was rather difficult waking up the next morning; I was shattered. The time we took having breakfast helped to get my poor, aching muscles moving again and then, we had barely time to roll up the sleeping bags, before the helicopter arrived to drop off the crew. I was pleased to see them but less happy to have to talk to the camera; I would need to make an effort not to say anything stupid. All the same, I said something silly: 'I was not expecting the summit to have such a sharp ridge. From below it looked flat.'

I told them how, as I climbed the mountain, I kept feeling as if I had done it before. The reason was that I had mentally prepared myself for meeting all kinds of difficulties and to expect the worst. So I was already anticipating everything that I came across, or rather I was ready to confront it, and it seemed that nothing could have properly put me off. That is why I was fine for the whole climb.

Then, as they always do after an ascent, they filmed my puffy hands which were so bad after working without gloves to protect them, and so swollen, that I could not bend my fingers properly. However, unlike on the Dru, they were not hurting at all. It would just take two or three days for the swelling to go down.

Once all the filming was done, Jeff and I started on the way down. We took a slight detour to the right to try and find his bag, but it seemed to have disappeared. Although selfish of me, it suited me that he did not find it. I was stiff all over and slightly dazed and did not see how I would be able to tie complicated knots to get it down.

Thanks to some long slides on our backsides, it took two hours to get down. Then, both ravenous, we stopped at the first restaurant we came across, at the railway station where we had slept the night before my departure, to wolf down an enormous steak and chips. With no ice cream on the menu and even less chance of finding profiteroles, the longed-for dessert would have to wait until later.

Back at the hotel, I had scarcely arrived when I was wanted on the telephone. It was Catherine Devaux, the agent who had been supporting me for a few months. After my ascent of the Dru, I was overwhelmed with all kinds of offers: for interviews, lectures, advertising, etc., and had called upon her to manage it all. It was therefore she who had been in charge of liaising with the media for the Eiger ascent, and she was calling to inform me about the timing of telephone interviews with the press.

It was all part of my work as a professional climber, but I would have preferred to spend the first minutes back in civilisation together with my friends. They needed to take the images back to Paris quickly and now I would not have a peaceful moment to talk to them.

My ascent hit the news – it was in newspapers all over the world. The Ogre was still in the public consciousness and, if the main headlines were anything to go by, she still had her dreadful reputation:

'Destivelle: KOs the Ogre.'[1]

'Destivelle, first woman to tame the fearsome North Face of the Eiger.'[2]

'Destivelle devours the Ogre.'[3]

'Smile of victory on the head of the Ogre.'[4]

As usual, I did not read any of the articles. Why not? Perhaps as a form of self protection. Journalists never repeat things the way they were actually said and the true facts are told either in a vague way, or full of exaggeration, both of which annoy and embarrass me because what they say does not reflect what I have actually gone through. I dislike it when they embellish things and am also upset by the potential reaction from people in the mountaineering world when reading stories; eulogies often as not, which are sometimes quite laughable. If I don't read them, I'm not upset by them. It's

1 *Le Figaro Magazine*, 14 March 1992.
2 *Sport Tonic*.
3 *L'Équipe*, 11 March 1992.
4 *Paris Match*.

probably a bit juvenile of me but it has helped me not to dwell on these things and to move on.

After the ascent of the Eiger, my peers deigned to acknowledge me and our relationship changed. Some congratulated me, others asked me to climb with them. I was very pleased with the recognition, which seemed to mean that maybe in their eyes I was no longer just the girl climber who was always in the news. I had become a true alpinist.

THE GRANDES JORASSES AND
THE MATTERHORN

All men dream: but not equally.
Those who dream by night in the dusty recesses
of their minds wake up in the day to find it was vanity,
but the dreamers of the day are dangerous men,
for they may act their dreams with open eyes,
to make it possible.
'*Seven Pillars of Wisdom: A Triumph*'
T. E. Lawrence, 1922.

While I was preparing for my ascent of the Eiger, dreams of
climbing other mythical routes floated into my head. I wanted
to treat myself to the north face of the Grandes Jorasses via
the Walker Spur and the north face of The Matterhorn via the
Schmid Brothers' route. In the post-war years, these faces
were thought of as the last major challenges of the Alps and
even nowadays, alpinists mention them in hushed tones. I
wanted to solo them during winter. The choice of season was
still primarily linked to safety, as on no account did I want to
be exposed to falling rocks; in winter everything is bonded together in the ice and there is less likelihood of other mountaineers being there. Climbers can inadvertently dislodge bits
of rock; climbing solo beneath them is unwise.

The other reason was that a winter ascent felt like a higher
prize, as difficulties are slightly increased; where the decision
to climb solo was concerned, the reason was more personal. I
absolutely love the sensation: with thoughts completely focused on the action, there is no room in my head for fear and
my moves are perfect and exact. I also like the feeling of
power and being totally in control that I have in these

situations. I can barely bring myself to admit the last reason, and I only realised recently on deep introspection – nobody can now say that it was my climbing partner, male of course, who did all the work. When I climbed the Yugoslavian route in the Trango Towers, I had to suffer unfair criticism of that nature. At the time I thought it insignificant but with hindsight, I realise that it irritated me deeply. In a way, these solo ascents would serve to heal my wounded pride.

For me, the biggest slice of the cake was the Eiger and having succeeded, I had the feeling that the other mountains would not be as satisfying since, even before starting on any preparation, I already thought myself up to the task. I was not too much in awe of the Grandes Jorasses as most of the route was on rock – my element – and the Matterhorn via the classic north face was reputed to be easier than the two others, and should not cause me any difficulty either. These projects were becoming less exciting but I was still keen to take them on and I decided that I would also have a bash at some very high altitude faces in the Himalaya. The timetable was: winter in the Alps and spring, summer or autumn, whichever was best, in the Himalaya.

These trips were rather expensive but my main sponsor allocated me a fairly large annual budget which allowed me to contemplate making a little expedition. The year I climbed the Eiger, the marketing director was so surprised and more relevantly so delighted with all the press coverage, that he saw an expedition as the cherry on top. If I came back empty-handed, it would not matter at all. You could say, he had already had his money's worth. This was fortunate, as being under pressure from sponsors is unsound, especially in the Himalaya where unforeseen problems, worse than in the Alps, considerably reduce the likelihood of success. Since my solo ascent of the Bonatti pillar in the Dru, I have always managed to avoid any pressure other than my own wish to do things.

The summer of that year, I went to Pakistan with Jeff Lowe to climb Latok 1. We planned to climb the 7,200 metre peak by the north east pillar, which Jeff had already attempted with a strong team of American climbers but had given up 100 metres from the summit. The route consisted of two parts: a rocky pillar 1,000 metres high, and then a long snow ridge going up for about 600 metres. I was excited about the second part, as it was something which I had not yet fully mastered. Unfortunately, bad weather and serious risk of avalanches prevented us from attempting it and forced us to turn back at 6,400 metres. It was the first time I had ever had to give up and I found it frustrating. As a salve to our conscience, we remembered what Shackleton said to his wife on his return, safe and sound from his attempt to reach the South Pole, 'Better a live ass than a dead lion.'

Quite apart from the fact that we returned empty handed, I do not have good memories of that expedition, which was stressful for the full two months it took. Firstly at base camp we were worried about bears. A few years before, some Japanese had had all their food taken in a single night; if that happened to us, the expedition would be over. But there was nothing we could do other than worry all the time, as we had no firearms. There was also the fact that I was anxious that the person in charge of organising our food and transport might turn up. Realising that we were being cheated over the contents of the cases, I had written them a furious letter. We were being charged for twelve bottles of ketchup, ten aerosol cans of mosquito repellent and plenty more... Jeff had told me, 'You should not have sent him that letter. In Pakistan they have different customs. You have questioned his honour and the man may well come to base camp to kill you.'

I don't know if he really meant what he said, but the result was that I had some suitably restless nights. I woke at the lightest sound and, as we were sleeping on a glacier, there were plenty of noises: falling stones, creaking ice... I prefer by far to sleep up on the face or to have an advance base camp two hours' hike from the foot of the pillar. Although even at that camp I had 48 hours of intense terror.

The day we were supposed to start climbing the second section of the route, bad weather threatened and we had to hastily descend the rock pillar, leaving our belay rope at the bergschrund to save time on the next attempt. We did not need it as our tent was on a dry glacier without snow, so that we could easily see any crevasses we needed to cross. That night, it snowed so hard that we had to go out several times to push the snow off the tent to prevent it from ripping. Then, at four or five in the morning, a rumbling woke us. Jeff shouted, 'Avalanche. Quick, get out!'

I was really not expecting this sort of thing. In a panic and without even putting on our boots, we rushed to shelter behind a small rock about one metre twenty in diameter; a paltry shelter but probably better than nothing. We had barely crouched down when an icy wind blew with unbelievable strength for a few seconds, then, nothing. The avalanche did not come as far as us. With my heart pounding and breathing hard, I asked Jeff what he thought.

'Well,' he replied calmly, 'I hope there's not another bigger one coming.'

How could he stay so calm? I was terrified. Our fate depended merely on luck. My stomach churning with fear, I spent the rest of the night with my boots on, listening out for any suspect noises. There were two false alerts when we need not have rushed out – the avalanche probably came down some way off.

The next morning we could not think of going down the glacier back to the other base camp without a rope, as the crevasses hidden by the new snow were death-traps. We had to wait two days until the storm was over and René Robert the photographer, roped up to the liaison officer, could come up to us. The wait was punctuated with having to rush outside at the sound of sinister rumblings. Fortunately, each time all that reached us was the wind. The one time the snow actually came as far as us, we did not leave the tent as we had been asleep and reacted too late to do anything other than await our fate.

Once again, luck was on our side, although pretty well squashed, the tent held against the wind and our sleeping bags just got a fine dusting of snow. Extremely happy to be alive, we cut our attempt on Latok 1 short and I practically ran home. The adventure proved to me the statistics on the likelihood of success in the Himalaya. Once back in France, for a while I savoured the luxury of a peaceful city dweller's existence. Once I had recovered, the next winter, I readied myself for an ascent of Les Jorasses via the Walker Spur. Just as for the other climbs, this project needed meticulous planning. I knew that, even solo, it would not be possible for me to climb it in one day as on the Eiger; so I would need bivvy gear. What that meant was that I would have to take a fairly heavy bag, too heavy to carry on my back whilst climbing. I would therefore need to belay most of the time.

I was ready in February. The day before I left, a girlfriend told me how anxious she was about my plans since, as far as she knew, no one had ever climbed that route solo in winter before. Only one or two teams had done it in winter conditions before and that had taken them several days. In fact, I had actually not checked that detail before, assuming that it was a classic route. In any case, I was not at all put off. I was confident and, unlike the way I felt just before setting off at the foot of the Eiger, did not feel as if I were about to take an exam. It must be said that the fact I had comfortable bivvy gear made a big difference, as it did not matter how long I spent on the face.

I reached the base of the route on cross country skis in the company of a few friends: Michel Pellé who had been with me on the Dru, René Robert and Bruno Robert a mountaineer friend. The latter was planning to solo climb the Croz Spur, and we had arranged to descend together to Courmayeur. His route being a little less arduous than mine, he would leave a day later. If he did not arrive in time, I was thinking of abseiling down via the Hirondelles ridge, as I did not on any account want to be alone on the glaciers on the Italian side.

To our great surprise, we met Lucien Berardini, known as 'Lulu' at the base of the Leschaux glacier. He is a famous alpinist who was very active in the 1950s and 1960s. He was especially well known for having been part of the great adventure on the south face of Aconcagua in 1954, together with his usual climbing partner Robert Paragot, where his hands and feet became seriously frozen and he lost several fingers and toes as a result.

Amazed to see him alone, I asked, 'Where are you off to?'

'You haven't seen a pony tail up there have you?' he replied in his thick Parisian accent, pointing up at the Grandes Jorasses, whose summit we could just see from where we were.

As usual he was joking, but this time his drawn face gave him away. Seeing our questioning faces, he explained that his 'buddy' Hugues Beauzile, a talented young cliff climber had gone off solo on the Walker Spur.

'The bloody idiot has no experience of mountains. I wonder how he is doing – we have had no radio contact since yesterday. A friend from the Leschaux Refuge says he saw his rasta ponytail bouncing about this morning.'

Then he talked for quite a while explaining what had pushed the young climber to attempt the Grandes Jorasses alone. It seemed that Hugues had done it because of a bet he had had with 'old Lulu'.

Devastated , he kept repeating, 'I never thought he would do it. Bloody hell, how could he be so stupid?'

I got the impression that he felt guilty for not having been able to stop him. Rather than going straight to the refuge, he came with us up the glacier as far as the bottom of the mountain.

When we got to the foot of the face, we prepared to bivouac overnight, as I wanted to be off early in the morning.

As we were unpacking our things, we suddenly heard Lulu shouting, 'Just look at that. The little idiot took his skis off on a snow bridge.

Lulu was right. There was a depression in the snow just where Hughes had left his skis. If the snow covering had given way under his weight, Hughes would have fallen into the crevasse. I gave a shiver of fear. If there is one thing that really scares me, it is crevasses. I cannot imagine why. It is a real phobia I cannot control, to the point where I have difficulty stepping over them, even when the gap is only ten centimetres, and when I get across at last, my heart is beating so hard that I am out of breath as if I had done a sprint. The same irrational fear grips me when entering a cave or a cellar without lights. Even if I have a torch I am so afraid, that alone it can take me hours to dare go in. If there is someone with me, I am not happy but can follow them. Each time, I know I am being ridiculous but am just incapable of overcoming my dread. On glaciers, I will not move one step if I am not roped to a companion.

Lulu left us to take his friend's skis to the refuge.

I did not lose a moment's sleep over the coming climb. I was surprised at being so calm as, for previous ascents, I had felt as if I were on starting blocks raring to go. This time, it was almost as if I were going off on an ordinary climb.

Michel belayed me over the bergschrund. He knew what I was like when it came to crevasses and, full of sympathy, did not make fun of me as I whimpered with terror at the edge of the gaping hole. He was also very patient, as it seemed to take me forever to get across by means of a narrow snow bridge, even though it was no more than five or six metres long. I crept across as if on eggshells, holding my breath at each step, afraid the vibration would shatter the thin snow I was standing on. After every step, legs quivering, I paused to check if my weight was not about to topple the structure, expecting at any moment to plummet with the snow into the chasm and become a dangling bundle over the enormous black hole. Then, when nothing happened, I tried to catch my breath and let out some of the paralysing stress. But standing there, I could not help but look down into the black hole and the horrible sight gave me rushes of adrenaline which did nothing to calm me.

It felt like a victory when I did eventually get across the awful abyss; I was quite proud of myself for being so brave. Crossing the bergschrund actually turned out to be the hardest part of the route for me, as the rest only involved technical difficulties.

Having thanked Michel for his help, I quickly climbed the first 200 metres of easy mixed terrain, pulling the rope behind me. Reaching the base of a 30 metre groove, I could see right away that it would not be sensible to climb it wearing a rucksack. So I relieved myself of my burden and belayed carefully. I was surprised at how hard that rock climbing section was. It was tougher than I had expected and I had to make a big effort to get across it properly. I was used to the grip of flexible climbing boots, and found climbing in big, rigid, mountaineering boots made me move awkwardly. I worried that my feet might slip, so I had to double check where to put my toes, trying to choose good, solid edges. Dictated as it was by footholds, this climb forced me into impossible and extremely tiring positions. As I concentrated, I appreciated the technique of the first men to master this face in 1938, as this section was frankly not easy. Once out of the groove, I secured my rope, went down to fetch my bag, and went back up with ascenders. The operation brought back old memories of the Dru.

At that point I was hoping there would not be too much rope work during this ascent. Unfortunately, I underestimated the route and, unavoidably, there was plenty more. From the groove on, the technical challenge of the sections proved too difficult to climb with a big bag, and I had to belay myself almost all the time. On occasion, I was really tempted to go without safety precautions, but not knowing what was in store just a few metres above, I did not dare. At times like that, I almost regretted having chosen to tackle this ascent alone. With a partner, the rope would have been much easier to handle and the climb would have gone more quickly … oh well, it was my decision and I was enjoying myself anyway.

It took three days to climb the magnificent, pillar of rock which is the 1,000 metre Walker Spur. I could probably have done it in two and a half if my alarm had gone off one morning and also stupidly getting lost. The two mistakes cost me five hours. Throughout the three days, the intense cold made the climb notable, with temperatures reaching -20°C. For the first time, I found my hands sticking to the rock like on a tray of ice cubes. That was one way of not slipping. I just had to make sure I did not leave any skin behind, though I was glad I am able to climb without gloves in such cold.

When I reached the summit, I was still happy to have succeeded, even if I were not overjoyed as on the Eiger. The route was truly beautiful, nevertheless, I told myself I would like to do the climb again in the summer wearing climbing boots, with a friend, as all the rigmarole of belaying had spoiled the fun a bit.

The next morning as planned, Bruno and I climbed back down on the Italian side. When we reached Courmayeur, an Italian guide told us that Hughes had had to call the rescue teams to get down from the last refuge as he was suffering from frostbite on his feet. We were very sorry to hear that, but felt that he had got away lightly, as we had been quite horrified to see his tracks on some enormous snow bridges. He was lucky not to fall down a crevasse.

Although the north face of the Grandes Jorasses is less well known outside mountaineering circles than the Eiger, my ascent nevertheless attracted excitement from the media. Hughes also deserved press coverage, but unfortunately, being a boy and unknown to non-climbers, he only merited a few lines here and there. It was unfair. Yet again, I was only too aware of the advantage of being a girl. After all, apart from the Dru, none of my ascents had been anything more than firsts for a woman. What was more, as time went on and my celebrity grew, the media could more easily talk about me. Even though I took advantage of it, to be comfortable with the way things were, I needed not to feel guilty about what I was doing.

If I had wanted to become even better known, I could have undertaken 'show-off climbs', like climbing the Eiffel Tower which I had once been given permission to do when I was on television. Had I done so, the fall out from the media would probably have become even greater no matter what mountains I climbed; but I could not care less about climbing the Eiffel Tower and I would just have felt like a performing monkey, not to mention the derision other climbers would have showered on me. To acquire fame through something that went against what I am looking for in life would have made me ill. I would rather be talked about as a real climber rather than as a puppet.

If my reputation had helped me follow my dreams, it had also isolated me. Of course I met many stimulating people but how to tell whether they were there for me or for what I represented? I no longer heard from my old friends and I was too embarrassed by what I had become to dare call them. Did they disapprove of my media image? Did they think I had forgotten them or was too much in demand to have time for them? The answer was no doubt a bit of everything mixed together. In truth, although I led a pretty exciting life, I frequently felt loneliness weighing heavily.

It was travel and expeditions which made me feel less isolated, as I went together with friends who shared my passion. As far as they were concerned, I was no longer just an image; I was no longer talking mountains, I was actually living them. Away from the journalists, the lectures, the autographs and all the other demands on my time, I was just a mountaineer amongst others the way it was before…

So that spring I went off on an expedition as if I were going on holiday. We were making for Makalu, the fourth highest summit in the world: 8,463 metres. Jeff wanted to climb solo to open a route on the west face which, despite several attempts, had never been done. Naively, I had suggested we

meet on the summit after I took the route opened by a French
team in 1971 on the West Pillar. We could then climb down
via the glacier slopes of the north face.

I was obviously not planning to go off alone on the route. I
would attempt it with a French alpinist who had a lot of experience of high altitude expeditions, Erik Decamp.

We had known each other for a long time, but had never
climbed together. He was also from Paris and had been part
of the little group of friends with whom I used to go to
Fontainebleau as a teenager and who had taught me so much.
The year I met them, Erik had just finished his studies at one
of the best universities and had left for Grenoble. Even though
he no longer climbed the Parisian rocks, I used to hear my
friends, or the specialised press, talking about his expeditions.
Our paths crossed from time to time at climbing exhibitions
or mountain climbing film festivals. After I opened the Dru
route, he had sent me a very nice note of congratulation which,
coming from him, was flattering, and touched me all the more
deeply, being the only one I received from a climber.

When I bumped into Erik by chance at a festival a few
months before going to Makalu, it seemed perfectly natural to
tell him all about my plans. It turned out that he too had
wanted to climb the West Pillar and suggested he come on the
expedition. I was pleased at the idea of attempting the ascent
with Erik. I trusted him; he was one of the people I classed as
'sound' in the mountains. He was not one of those hotheads
who will risk their lives for a summit – and it was no bad thing
that I found him easy to talk to about other stuff too…

On this particular expedition, I invited my mother to come
with us as far as base camp. This was the first time we were
going off on a real journey together and I was especially
pleased as I had long wanted to show her Nepal; with its sherpas, the mountain life, the way time seems to move, the pleasure of walking and to show her that expeditions were not
uninterrupted nightmares. In short, I wanted to introduce her

to the world I love so much.

The hike to base camp was made quite difficult by bad weather and took fourteen days, of which the last four were the worst as we suffered violent snowstorms. This was not exactly what I had hoped for my mother's first experience, but nothing seemed to dispel her good humour. It seemed that her confidence in us and especially in Erik, helped her overcome the ordeals. When we had to shelter in a cave; huddled around a miserable fire, pathetic and soaked, while we waited for porters; rather than complain, she laughed at the humour in the situation and continued to chat away as if nothing were amiss. I was impressed by her ability to adapt to new and uncomfortable situations.

Once we arrived at the base camp, despite the altitude and her inexperience, she bounced around better than us and behaved as she did at home. She did not stop: helping the sherpas prepare meals, sewing my sponsors' logos onto the rucksacks, organising the provisions, etc. Having six children had not accustomed her to sitting around and not working.

She only stayed two days at base camp and, when she left, I found it quite hard. As we said our goodbyes I was heartbroken and had to make a big effort not to show how I felt. As soon as her back was turned, I dived into my tent to hide my tears. I had loved having her with me and it worried me to see her leave alone; I felt bad at having dragged her into such a hostile environment. Of course she was not really alone, as Kami, a porter and Christine Grosjean, a friend of mine were with her, but it bothered me not to be there too. I felt responsible for her.

The thought of Kami, whom I had instructed to look after her since the start, was reassuring. I had watched him throughout our hike and thought him very vigilant; if my mother slipped while he was walking a metre or two behind her, he would leap forward to catch her arm and, at the slightest sign of fatigue, he carried her bag. We nicknamed him the 'guardian angel'. What a character he was. He constantly recited prayers and whenever he washed his rosary, made of seeds, he asked us to watch over it as it dried, to protect it from birds.

The loveliest memories I have from my travels in Nepal are from going through villages. Different thoughts and sensations are evoked by human life, rather than nature on its own. In the same way, just back from an expedition, it feels marvellous to return to humanity. I have never climbed to get away from it all. I climb with people; it is they who help me learn and feel. When I come up against bad weather or difficulties on a face, I cope precisely because I have people to return to who love me. I cannot even imagine going off climbing in a huff or to escape.

I don't think I would ever want to go climbing with alpinists with whom I do not get on, as I enjoy the company as much as the climb. That is why I have never agreed to go on major expeditions; I am not interested in the summit just for its own sake.

At Makalu I was trying out being at very high altitudes and found it slowed me down, mentally as well as physically. Although to be expected, the effects of the altitude upset me as I realised that, if problems arose, I was not sure I would be physically up to them and my partner too would be weakened by the lack of oxygen. I found our vulnerability worrying and it spoiled the fun of the climb a little. For the first time in my career as a mountaineer, I was glad of the bad weather which prevented me from climbing. Well, actually not entirely, there was still part of me frustrated at being deprived of a summit, while the other part was saying, 'Good, it's over now, enough discomfort, let's go home quickly.'

With hindsight, I thought it was too ambitious to want to climb the pillar in Alpine style – just two climbers with no porters or fixed ropes – and resolved in future to attempt lower summits. It is of no interest to me to climb above 8,000 metres for its own sake; what attracts me is the technical difficulty of a climb and I would prefer not to do a summit at all rather than reach it via an uninteresting route.

To cut straight to the question, 'What about Everest?' The answer is that, although to be able to list the highest mountain in the world among my achievements would be nice, as I am unable to climb it via a difficult route without oxygen, I am simply not interested. That is of course pretentious but what I like doing is succeeding on routes that few mountaineers are capable of climbing. Difficult goals make me surpass myself.

Though none of the expedition made the summit of Makalu – even Jeff had to give up – I left full of beans. I had got to know Erik, who was to become my companion and a bit later, the father of our child, Victor.

On my return, I decided to put the finishing touches to my last project: to climb the most famous and perhaps the most beautiful mountain in the world, the Matterhorn.

I was no longer interested in the classic north face route, the Schmid. I was looking for one which, if not more difficult, would at least require careful preparation and a certain amount of concentration. I find it so much more enjoyable when I am not quite sure whether I will succeed.

On that count Les Grandes Jorasses had been frustrating. The Matterhorn route I chose was the one Bonatti had opened, alone, in 1965 to commemorate the very first ascent of the mountain. It took him five days of hard labour to reach the summit. It appeared that no one had repeated the route although several major names in the mountaineering world had come a cropper on it. Was that due to bad weather, or was it really hard? Perhaps they had given up simply because they were not interested in the line which does not go straight up. Some of the time, I thought I did not need to know the reasons and reckoned that, with a bit of effort, I had a chance of success.

Bonatti was a very good climber, but in 30 years, climbing had progressed enormously, and there was no reason for me not to succeed. At other times, not knowing why others had failed worried me. Was I not over-estimating my ability? The alpinists who had attempted it were really very good. I took to reading Walter Bonatti's accounts, which I did not find reassuring either; he had treated the ascent as a battle and did not seem to have enjoyed it at all.

Then I bought, from a specialist collector of articles and books about mountaineering, the issue of *Paris Match* in which the event was reported. There were black and white photos, taken from an airplane during his ascent. That surprised me. So it was not just my generation which organised media coverage in order to live from our passion. Walter Bonatti seemed far from a novice in this approach. He had even taken photos while on the face; especially one of his bag with his mascot Zizi, a little teddy bear, attached to it. On that point he had certainly beaten me. I have never managed to take a photo while solo climbing, although I have been encouraged to do so and have even taken up a camera, but I forget or cannot be bothered.

I learned from the article that I would not find a platform on which to bivouac and that it would be hard to put in pitons. So like Bonatti, I would use a hammock. Ready at last, I left for Zermatt with Erik who would climb the Schmid brothers' route and meet me at the summit. I was a little tense, wondering what difficulties lay ahead.

The day before I started, Erik and I went to reconnoitre the approach and, to spare myself the stress of the black hole the next day, I took the opportunity to put a rope across the bergschrund.

At the refuge that evening I tried to behave as if I was going to do something quite ordinary. I did not want to worry Erik who was in an awkward position: he must have been worried about my project but, respecting me, did not feel he had the right to hold me back. He said then and has always said since, 'If that's what you want to do, you do it.'

He did not encourage me but neither did he dissuade me – the decision was mine. That evening I felt I was being a selfish beast. It wasn't very nice to bring him into this. We could have done the climb together. If the roles were reversed, I would be anxious; but he did not show it and I was grateful to him.

Although I did not tell him, I had a knot in the pit of my stomach. The only thing that vaguely eased my conscience was that he had decided to take the Schmid route – so we had a project each.

I was at the foot of the route at nine in the morning. As I said goodbye to Erik, I felt a stab of remorse for leaving him behind. The anguish was short-lived when, as we hugged, I saw a wide grin showing his approval. He did not look a bit put out and even seemed rather pleased. With that, reassured by his attitude, I quickly cheered up and my thoughts turned to action. To function at my best, I needed to feel that he did not mind and even approved of my decision to climb solo. What did he really think? It was timely that what I saw let me set off up the route with a clear conscience.

Once past the bergschrund with my fixed rope, I turned and we gave each other a last wave. Erik would not be setting off on the other route for another two days.

The little worries about my love life had made me lose the thread of my thoughts but it was now time to stop daydreaming. To get my full concentration back, I took a while sorting my equipment. Carefully putting everything into its usual place, my spirits rose and I was keen to climb again. I got down to the business of the ascent. The rock climbing was tricky without being difficult, on hard rock which meant it was not really possible to belay, as the opportunities to put in pitons were few and far between and for nuts and Friends nonexistent. It felt as if I were climbing without any protection.

What was more, where the wind had caused snow to collect under little overhangs, it made big white mushrooms which blocked the route every five metres. It took a lot of concentration each time I needed to get past one, as the unstable snow was only too ready to give way. I tried to remove some to access a more solid surface, but it needed care, as I was afraid that the clumps of snow might unbalance me as they fell. Absorbed by what I was doing, I did not notice time passing until I started to feel tired, at which point I looked up. I was beginning to be fed up with having to concentrate so hard and was dismayed and a bit anxious to see that there was plenty more of this.

It was already four o'clock, the light would soon be going and nightfall was in two hours. That did not leave much time to leave this section and find somewhere to bivouac. Where I was, it was impossible to secure a hammock to the rock and, even though in winter everything is held by ice, I still thought this place was too prone to falling rocks. I had something to eat and drink while I thought, as I had eaten nothing since the start, which probably accounted for my fatigue. I left that first 200 metre wall at around six to find myself on ice. It was a relief to be able to lower my guard a little but as night approached, I became increasingly anxious; the slope was fairly steep and there was still nowhere to bivouac. Setting up in the middle of an ice slope made no sense. I wanted somewhere flat even if very narrow, just so that I could put my feet down.

I briefly considered cutting a step into the ice but all the hard work would not guarantee a comfortable night. As I went on, panic started to gnaw. It was essential that I find a solution before dark. Reaching a hillock of fresh snow, I realised I had found it, here under my nose but that my mind, dulled by fatigue and stress had taken a while to notice. What I had to do was dig a platform in the snow.

Without wasting any time I got on with it and then set up my bivouac shelter, a teepee shaped bag whose point at the top was held in the snow with an ice axe. As the slope was not very steep, the fabric on the downhill side would probably flap into my face all night, but at least the base would be flat. I protected it all by securing the rope twenty metres above in some rock and then, pleased with my sleeping arrangements, I set about taking out all the bivvy paraphernalia. When I opened my rucksack, a green bag slipped out and plummeted down the mountain. Powerless to stop it, I watched it disappearing into the abyss. Aghast, without even trying to think what it contained, my first reaction was, 'It's over.'

I could not see how I was to carry on without every bit of the gear I had planned to take, but was furious about giving up – what a stupid mistake. I must admit that I did not mind the idea of stopping there too much. The progress I had made that day had been tedious, I felt slow and low on energy; not really with it at all. Losing the bag might be a good excuse to turn back. I quickly pulled myself together, telling myself that the bag might not contain anything really essential and with a bit of luck I might be able to carry on.

When I unpacked all my other things, to my delight, I discovered there was nothing absolutely essential: I had lost a toothbrush, a mini-tube of toothpaste, a tiny bar of soap, aspirin, my warmest gloves and spare batteries for the headlamp. That upset me psychologically, as I appreciate a bit of comfort; but the damage was very slight. I still had two pairs of gloves, albeit less warm but, as I can stand the cold, I wouldn't much miss the warmest ones. As for the batteries; I would just have to use less light.

That evening I melted snow for water in the dark, only switching on the torch briefly to find the ingredients for my meal. To replenish my energy levels, I forced down soup, mashed potato and ham and then called Erik on the radio. It did me good to tell him about my mishap; it made it seem less of a drama. He reassured me about the weather forecast: the sky had clouded over in the middle of the day and I had wondered what was in store.

Once I was comfortably installed in my sleeping bag, I tried to get to sleep. I usually drop off without any problem but that night I couldn't as I didn't feel very well. An hour later, a violent urge to vomit catapulted me from my shelter. Having turned myself inside out just beyond the entrance, I crawled back into the tent feeling very sorry for myself. This time I really did think it was all over: I would climb back down.

Only, just then, I was incapable of doing anything. To descend safely, I would have to get better. I made myself drink and eat but could only keep down dried fruit; not much, just one or two raisins at a time, though I slept so badly, that I was able to eat a little every hour. Little by little, I felt better and when I woke in the morning I was more or less well, though not in the best of moods. It would not be a problem to climb down. When at last I poked my head out, my mood was radically changed by the sight of the rock. The rocks above me seemed like a lover calling to me, so, obeying instinct, I changed my mind and carried on up. I spent that second day, really pleased to be there, on the Traversée des Anges. To describe it, I could almost quote Walter Bonatti directly from *Montagnes d'une Vie*[1] :

Its rocks are extremely smooth and hard and will take but few pitons which are never very secure; furthermore they incline so steeply that I am pushed to the limits of my equilibrium. [I would just have said that it was a demanding climb].

The Traversée des Anges is clothed in a mantel of unstable snow, which I must clear at each pace. If only Panei had forgotten to remove the few pitons I had succeeded in placing with such difficulty. [He had already attempted the climb with a partner but, due to poor weather had been forced back; and in my description, I could have substituted, 'If only Bonatti had forgotten to remove his pitons!']

There are 120 almost horizontal metres of traverse, on slabs which are very steep, icy and barely sound. It is precisely for angels that it is good. [I would not have said 'barely sound', and would never have thought of angels]

These slabs occupy me until the evening and I advance with the utmost care inching along, putting in rare pitons, which serve better to ease the mind than to secure the rope. Then, I return to load the bag onto my shoulders, a bag which seems to get heavier and heavier. To sum up, my progress is always in the same fashion, be it forwards or backwards but, as I traverse, I cannot use the rope to take my weight.

---

1. Arthaud, 1997.

Unlike Bonatti, I had a few extra tricks up my sleeve which he did not – for a start, nuts and Friends didn't exist in his time; it was a great relief to be able to use them two or three times on the traverse. In addition, my equipment, made of modern materials, was much lighter and more efficient than his. To give an example, in 1965, clothes were thicker, heavier, less flexible and less comfortable to move in than the synthetic fibres used nowadays which stretch, are waterproof, breathable and have warm fleeces. Personally, I have never suffered from the cold the way one reads about in mountaineering accounts before the 1970s. Furthermore, the materials of which climbing equipment is manufactured have become considerably lighter – for example krabs are now much better, made with aluminium rather than steel. My bag must have weighed a good ten kilos less than his. Finally, and I think this is the key point, I had the benefit of three decades of progress. Bonatti was a pioneer.

At the end of the Traversée des Anges, I found an indistinct little ledge, protected by an overhang. Despite the remaining hour and a half of daylight, I decided to stay there because, although uncomfortable, it had the advantage of being protected from falling rocks and I knew that I would find nothing as safe above the overhang. I was also keen not to overdo it. The day had gone well; I had enjoyed myself and did not want to spoil it all by pushing myself to the point where I felt at death's door as I had the day before.

I was rewarded for being so sensible and I managed to hang my hammock. The operation took a while, as it took quite some tinkering and careful adjustment to make it hold fast in a little dip. For once, I was glad I was small. I could now avoid a night spent like a fakir with the sharp stones of the ledge digging into my back. Bonatti, who was well built, wrote, 'I bivouacked squatting on a sort of step, suspended right in the middle of the vertical desert.' The place was indeed impressive hanging as it was over the face of the mountain.

As soon as I was tucked into my sleeping bag, not a little proud of suspending my hammock in such a clever way, I called Erik to tell him how comfortable I was and that all was going well. Things were fine with him too; the weather forecast was good and he would set off on his route in the morning.

That evening, the same things were on the menu as the previous one but I ate with relish. Then, replete, I slept like a baby until, in the middle of the night, I was rudely awakened by the sound so dreaded by all alpinists: the whistling of a rockfall. It seemed to pass right above my head. I was not afraid as I knew I was sheltered. I would need to take extra care for the next bivouac, since I was unlikely to find anywhere as well protected on the face above me.

The alarm on my watch went off at five thirty the next morning. I immediately lit the stove hanging in front of me and then lay back to treat myself to a few minutes' extra rest, while the water heated. Ten minutes later, I ate a sort of porridge of cereals, milk and chocolate powder and drank half a litre of tea. While I am climbing, I am never very hungry in the mornings but it was essential to have a nourishing breakfast, since I had a long day ahead, and would have few opportunities to eat anything, all the more so as I often forget to eat when I am in action.

As the lights of Zermatt were melting away into the glimmers of the dawning day, I set off up the big overhang above me. It was seven o'clock. Climbing those ten metres of rock was magnificent: I hung out into the air from excellent, big holds. At one point, as I looked down on the face in search of footholds, my attention was caught by a little black dot, moving way down below me. It was Erik. He was climbing the long ice slope at the foot of the Schmid route. I thought, 'Oh good, he's making good time.' I was happy that we were both having the same experience at the same time. It made me feel as if I was with him.

After the overhang, the face became less steep. It was made up of hard slabs, interspersed with crumbling rock and ice; the climbing got tricky again, putting in protection became difficult if not impossible, as it had been lower down. But now I was resigned to it and just moved gently along as for a solo climb. That way I climbed 300 metres.

Then, knowing that finding a place to bivouac would not be easy, at around four in the afternoon, I started to look carefully at the face around me. It was all depressingly flat, not the slightest little ledge, not the slightest step: just the slope. Although I climbed on higher and higher, still nothing. I started to get tired and to feel my concentration waning. So, when I reached a sort of round bulge at around six, I was losing hope and decided, against my better judgement to settle there. With a bit of luck, no rocks would fall but, if they did, the indistinct, stomach-shaped lump would afford some protection. In any case, there was no other option. I was exhausted and would certainly not find anything better unless I reached the summit, which was still several pitches away.

Without losing any time I put in several pitons, linked them together to spread the load and strung my hammock from them. This time, the bivouac would not win any prizes for comfort. I would be bundled up, squashed against the icy slope. Before settling down, I tried calling Erik. The mountain's contours had prevented us from seeing each other again. He was doing fine – now at the same altitude as me but two or three hundred metres to my left – he too was getting ready for the night. Hearing his voice made me want to cry. I hated the fact that he was so far from me. It would have been so good to meet here. We signed off saying, 'See you tomorrow at the summit.'

My bivouac was not that bad. In any case it did not prevent me from having a good night's sleep, but it was a painful awakening. As with every winter ascent, my hands were hurting. I had not once worn gloves since the start, to get a better grip on the holds. To add insult to injury, I had viciously cut a finger instead of some butter to improve my mashed potato. But, it was not very bad as, by the time I had eaten breakfast and packed up, I no longer noticed it. Now that the pain had gone, I was feeling cheerful and energetic as I resumed my climb; the summit and our reunion were close. Three or four pitches further up, I saw Erik at last. He was only about 100 metres from me. If all had gone according to plan, we would not have been that close. Had he gone too far to the right or me to the left? Or had we both slightly headed in each other's direction to meet up? It no longer mattered much – at this level, the terrain was identical. A 150 metres from the summit, we hugged at last. I was quite overcome and unable to hold back a few tears.

We decided to continue together and so, walking one behind the other, we reached the summit at around four in the afternoon. As it was too late to consider climbing down that evening, we slept on the summit of Cervin and celebrated our ascents in a dignified fashion. Erik surprised me by producing from his bag a bar of Swiss chocolate filled with pear liqueur, carried up especially for the occasion. Never had chocolate tasted so good! The next morning, we quickly climbed down via the east face, which fortunately had plenty of snow on it. At the bottom there was the photographer Pascal Tournaire, waiting to surprise us with his arms filled with pastries.

CONCLUSION

Definition – Mountaineering is the art of going all over mountains while confronting the greatest dangers with the greatest caution. We call art here the achievement of knowledge by means of action.

R. Daumal

With the ascent of The Matterhorn, whose success followed the one on the North Face of the Eiger and the Grandes Jorasses, I achieved the goal I had set myself.

I do not do many major climbs which really leave their mark on me as those did, be it solo or in a team – about one a year, if that. It took me three years to climb those three mountains. I both like and need to take my time to digest each ascent. One major project from time to time is enough to satisfy me completely. Besides, my whole life is not just about climbing mountains – I do not want to climb all the time, or to collect routes – that would make me think I was going nowhere. I need to occupy my mind with more than just climbing moves and have other activities.

I do admire the energy of some alpinists whose lives seem to be entirely devoted to their passion, and who ceaselessly climb race after race and face after face – and I know that when prevented from going out by the weather, they will be in a vile mood – but it is not what I seek. That sometimes makes me feel an outsider in my world since, even if I do not climb every day, I do not miss it. If I were forced to go, it would be to no avail, I would stop enjoying it and would then have neither the motivation nor the energy needed to throw myself fully into the projects on which I set my heart.

An ascent can appeal to me for a great variety of reasons. Often, the route and the summit conjure up a dream I entertained in my childhood or adolescence. At other times, it is about something new in comparison to what I have already accomplished. But to go from an appealing idea to a real project does not happen immediately. First of all, I need to think about it very deeply, to make the idea part of me, and not to be afraid of it. During this reflective phase, which can be quite long – taking between a few months and several years – I try to visualise all the dangers and technical challenges I could encounter. That encompasses the approach hike and the descent. I go about researching the climb, by discretely asking questions of other alpinists, reading books and articles. I try not to talk too much about my ideas, as I worry that I will be influenced one way or the other, if not appear pretentious.

Once the problems are clearly set out, and they seem reasonable and without great danger, the wish evolves into a real project. From then on the real preparation can begin. The time this stage takes can vary; depending on what type of climbing is needed and how fit I want to be, on the climatic conditions and whether I feel mentally ready. To be ready psychologically, I mean to feel good in myself, to have nothing bothering or annoying me. Many mountaineers give me the impression that they go climbing as a form of escape; that greatly frustrated by something, they head for the heights of the world in an attempt to resolve their problems. That could not be further from my state of mind. I need to be at peace with myself to be able to give the greatest attention to my climbing and do it properly. At this stage, I feel as if I were gently winding an internal spring, which I release when everything appears to be under control. Then, nothing other than real danger, as seen from an unbiased perspective can stop me. I feel strong, determined and almost invulnerable, with no doubts about my ability to succeed, and very happy to set off at last.

The part I like best is the actual climbing. I experience real pleasure when I am finally at the start of a climb, the minute planning is over, and all that remains is the action. I am as excited as a child with a new toy at the foot of each face, looking forward to touching the rock and deciphering the face all the way to the summit. While climbing, in contrast with almost anything else, I think exclusively about what I am doing and my thoughts and actions become one. This is what I like about climbing and what I liked right from the start when I was a child. You do not watch yourself climbing, you go into action and, if you value your life, you do not do it in any old way; you need to think, anticipate, manage your energy... It is this tactical game pitted against the elements which I love above all; the way of taking calculated risks which never stops being a great adventure and makes me challenge myself every time.

Now I have a child, Victor, the balance of my life is different. It is more important for me to be with him than on a climb; so I go away less often, although my love for climbing and going into the mountains has not diminished.

I still dream of famous mountains and high peaks and, even if I am less able to take it on, I still get the same excitement from letting the idea of a new project germinate and grow. When reliving some of my climbs to write about them, I found all the memories still inside me: moments of great fear, intense pleasure, sometimes suffering, weariness, anger and doubts. I could not say precisely what drives me to seek out these situations or to link my life so strongly to the mountains. For me it just seems right, without being able to tell what part is played by physical pleasure, confronting the elements, the beauty of the scenery, being put to the test, surpassing myself or the excitement at taking up a challenge. Some of the forces which motivated me have undoubtedly evolved with time.

Whether consciously or not, I most likely have a need to 'prove' something to myself certainly as a mountaineer, or as a woman, maybe to my parents? Who can tell? For me to feel well-balanced, I certainly need action and I find the enthusiasm of constantly doing new things and breaking new barriers stimulating. For whatever the reason, mountain climbing lets me develop and grow. It fills my life without being an obsession and I owe that life balance to the precious help I get from those around me, from friends and family. I have been lucky enough to have a talent for getting the best out of the help I have had in life, and to benefit from my surroundings and circumstances in order to make all my dreams come true. It is now down to me to give in return.

I enjoy sharing what I have experienced, as a technical adviser, lecturer and even in writing this book. If my audiences – be they business or individuals with a passion for adventure – find something to nourish their thoughts or dreams from my tales, I feel as if I am still making progress, still making more sense of my climbs and getting to know myself better.

What touches me most deeply are the days I spend showing children, especially my own little boy, the things I was lucky enough to experience as a child. Those days of discovery for, for me truly magical. They play in mountain streams, run in alpine pastures, learn about animals and wild flowers, eat wild strawberries, raspberries and blueberries, collect 'precious' stones (crystal, quartz and mica), go up to a refuge or a lake, go camping, walk on snow in the middle of summer – for them too, all these things are a source of incredible wonder. What a pleasure it is too, to see them on the rocks, getting pleasure from concentrating hard to overcome their fears, managing to make the right moves to get them to the top with a smile of triumph. As I have done, the children will remember those experiences their whole lives, and in my opinion, that is what matters most.

ROCK QUEEN